ISBN 0-8373-0799-6

C-799   CAREER EXAMINATION SERIES

This is your
PASSBOOK® for...

School Custodian

Test Preparation Study Guide

Questions & Answers

NLC

NATIONAL LEARNING CORPORATION

PASSBOOK®
NOTICE

PASSBOOK® SERIES

THE *PASSBOOK® SERIES* has been created to prepare applicants and candidates for the ultimate academic battlefield — the examination room.

At some time in our lives, each and every one of us may be required to take an examination — for validation, matriculation, admission, qualification, registration, certification, or licensure.

Based on the assumption that every applicant or candidate has met the basic formal educational standards, has taken the required number of courses, and read the necessary texts, the *PASSBOOK® SERIES* furnishes the one special preparation which may assure passing with confidence, instead of failing with insecurity. Examination questions — together with answers — are furnished as the basic vehicle for study so that the mysteries of the examination and its compounding difficulties may be eliminated or diminished by a sure method.

This book is meant to help you pass your examination provided that you qualify and are serious in your objective.

The entire field is reviewed through the huge store of content information which is succinctly presented through a provocative and challenging approach — the question-and-answer method.

A climate of success is established by furnishing the correct answers at the end of each test.

You soon learn to recognize types of questions, forms of questions, and patterns of questioning. You may even begin to anticipate expected outcomes.

You perceive that many questions are repeated or adapted so that you can gain acute insights, which may enable you to score many sure points.

You learn how to confront new questions, or types of questions, and to attack them confidently and work out the correct answers.

You note objectives and emphases, and recognize pitfalls and dangers, so that you may make positive educational adjustments.

Moreover, you are kept fully informed in relation to new concepts, methods, practices, and directions in the field.

You discover that you are actually taking the examination all the time: you are preparing for the examination by "taking" an examination, not by reading extraneous and/or supererogatory textbooks.

In short, this PASSBOOK®, used directedly, should be an important factor in helping you to pass your test.

SCHOOL CUSTODIAN

DUTIES AND RESPONSIBILITIES

Under general supervision, supervises and is reponsible for the physical operation, maintenance, repair, and custodial upkeep and care of a public school building and its immediate grounds; performs related work.

EXAMPLES OF TYPICAL TASKS

Supervises, plans and is responsible for the work of the custodial and maintenance staff. Heats building by means of low pressure boilers. Makes minor repairs to steam plant, heating equipment, electrical equipment, plumbing, structure, glazing and furniture. Supervises cleaning of the building and grounds. Is responsible for maintaining the building and grounds in a safe, secure and sanitary condition. Conducts inspection of building to determine needed repairs. Consults with and advises officials on problems of operation, maintenance and repairs. Sets up the work-schedules to insure maximum efficiency and minimum interference with classroom activities. Requisi tions and accounts for custodial and maintenance materials, tools and supplies. Maintains records and prepares required reports of plant operations. Hires appropriate personnel; trains or arranges for their training. For hired personnel, prepares payrolls and personnel forms, pays wages, and provides Workmen's Compensation Insurance.

SCOPE OF THE EXAMINATION

The written test will be of the multiple-choice type and may include questions on supervision of cleaning and maintenance of school buildings and grounds; operation and maintenance of heating and ventilating systems; inspection of buildings and grounds; reports and correspondence; public relations; safety and security; staff development; and other related areas.

HOW TO TAKE A TEST

I. YOU MUST PASS AN EXAMINATION

A. *WHAT EVERY CANDIDATE SHOULD KNOW*

Examination applicants often ask us for help in preparing for the written test. What can I study in advance? What kinds of questions will be asked? How will the test be given? How will the papers be graded?

As an applicant for a civil service examination, you may be wondering about some of these things. Our purpose here is to suggest effective methods of advance study and to describe civil service examinations.

Your chances for success on this examination can be increased if you know how to prepare. Those "pre-examination jitters" can be reduced if you know what to expect. You can even experience an adventure in good citizenship if you know why civil service exams are given.

B. *WHY ARE CIVIL SERVICE EXAMINATIONS GIVEN?*

Civil service examinations are important to you in two ways. As a citizen, you want public jobs filled by employees who know how to do their work. As a job seeker, you want a fair chance to compete for that job on an equal footing with other candidates. The best-known means of accomplishing this two-fold goal is the competitive examination.

Exams are widely publicized throughout the nation. They may be administered for jobs in federal, state, city, municipal, town or village governments or agencies.

Any citizen may apply, with some limitations, such as the age or residence of applicants. Your experience and education may be reviewed to see whether you meet the requirements for the particular examination. When these requirements exist, they are reasonable and applied consistently to all applicants. Thus, a competitive examination may cause you some uneasiness now, but it is your privilege and safeguard.

C. *HOW ARE CIVIL SERVICE EXAMS DEVELOPED?*

Examinations are carefully written by trained technicians who are specialists in the field known as "psychological measurement," in consultation with recognized authorities in the field of work that the test will cover. These experts recommend the subject matter areas or skills to be tested; only those knowledges or skills important to your success on the job are included. The most reliable books and source materials available are used as references. Together, the experts and technicians judge the difficulty level of the questions.

Test technicians know how to phrase questions so that the problem is clearly stated. Their ethics do not permit "trick" or "catch" questions. Questions may have been tried out on sample groups, or subjected to statistical analysis, to determine their usefulness.

Written tests are often used in combination with performance tests, ratings of training and experience, and oral interviews. All of these measures combine to form the best-known means of finding the right person for the right job.

II. HOW TO PASS THE WRITTEN TEST

A. NATURE OF THE EXAMINATION

To prepare intelligently for civil service examinations, you should know how they differ from school examinations you have taken. In school you were assigned certain definite pages to read or subjects to cover. The examination questions were quite detailed and usually emphasized memory. Civil service exams, on the other hand, try to discover your present ability to perform the duties of a position, plus your potentiality to learn these duties. In other words, a civil service exam attempts to predict how successful you will be. Questions cover such a broad area that they cannot be as minute and detailed as school exam questions.

In the public service similar kinds of work, or positions, are grouped together in one "class." This process is known as *position-classification*. All the positions in a class are paid according to the salary range for that class. One class title covers all of these positions, and they are all tested by the same examination.

B. FOUR BASIC STEPS

1) Study the announcement

How, then, can you know what subjects to study? Our best answer is: "Learn as much as possible about the class of positions for which you've applied." The exam will test the knowledge, skills and abilities needed to do the work.

Your most valuable source of information about the position you want is the official exam announcement. This announcement lists the training and experience qualifications. Check these standards and apply only if you come reasonably close to meeting them.

The brief description of the position in the examination announcement offers some clues to the subjects which will be tested. Think about the job itself. Review the duties in your mind. Can you perform them, or are there some in which you are rusty? Fill in the blank spots in your preparation.

Many jurisdictions preview the written test in the exam announcement by including a section called "Knowledge and Abilities Required," "Scope of the Examination," or some similar heading. Here you will find out specifically what fields will be tested.

2) Review your own background

Once you learn in general what the position is all about, and what you need to know to do the work, ask yourself which subjects you already know fairly well and which need improvement. You may wonder whether to concentrate on improving your strong areas or on building some background in your fields of weakness. When the announcement has specified "some knowledge" or "considerable knowledge," or has used adjectives like "beginning principles of..." or "advanced ... methods," you can get a clue as to the number and difficulty of questions to be asked in any given field. More questions, and hence broader coverage, would be included for those subjects which are more important in the work. Now weigh your strengths and weaknesses against the job requirements and prepare accordingly.

3) Determine the level of the position

Another way to tell how intensively you should prepare is to understand the level of the job for which you are applying. Is it the entering level? In other words, is this the position in which beginners in a field of work are hired? Or is it an intermediate or advanced level? Sometimes this is indicated by such words as "Junior" or "Senior" in the class title. Other jurisdictions use Roman numerals to designate the level – Clerk I, Clerk II, for example. The word "Supervisor" sometimes appears in the title. If the level is not indicated by the title, check the description of duties. Will you be working under very close supervision, or will you have responsibility for independent decisions in this work?

4) Choose appropriate study materials

Now that you know the subjects to be examined and the relative amount of each subject to be covered, you can choose suitable study materials. For beginning level jobs, or even advanced ones, if you have a pronounced weakness in some aspect of your training, read a modern, standard textbook in that field. Be sure it is up to date and has general coverage. Such books are normally available at your library, and the librarian will be glad to help you locate one. For entry-level positions, questions of appropriate difficulty are chosen – neither highly advanced questions, nor those too simple. Such questions require careful thought but not advanced training.

If the position for which you are applying is technical or advanced, you will read more advanced, specialized material. If you are already familiar with the basic principles of your field, elementary textbooks would waste your time. Concentrate on advanced textbooks and technical periodicals. Think through the concepts and review difficult problems in your field.

These are all general sources. You can get more ideas on your own initiative, following these leads. For example, training manuals and publications of the government agency which employs workers in your field can be useful, particularly for technical and professional positions. A letter or visit to the government department involved may result in more specific study suggestions, and certainly will provide you with a more definite idea of the exact nature of the position you are seeking.

III. KINDS OF TESTS

Tests are used for purposes other than measuring knowledge and ability to perform specified duties. For some positions, it is equally important to test ability to make adjustments to new situations or to profit from training. In others, basic mental abilities not dependent on information are essential. Questions which test these things may not appear as pertinent to the duties of the position as those which test for knowledge and information. Yet they are often highly important parts of a fair examination. For very general questions, it is almost impossible to help you direct your study efforts. What we can do is to point out some of the more common of these general abilities needed in public service positions and describe some typical questions.

1) General information

Broad, general information has been found useful for predicting job success in some kinds of work. This is tested in a variety of ways, from vocabulary lists to questions about current events. Basic background in some field of work, such as sociology or economics, may be sampled in a group of questions. Often these are principles which have become familiar to most persons through exposure rather than through formal training. It is difficult to advise you how to study for these questions; being alert to the world around you is our best suggestion.

2) Verbal ability

An example of an ability needed in many positions is verbal or language ability. Verbal ability is, in brief, the ability to use and understand words. Vocabulary and grammar tests are typical measures of this ability. Reading comprehension or paragraph interpretation questions are common in many kinds of civil service tests. You are given a paragraph of written material and asked to find its central meaning.

3) Numerical ability

Number skills can be tested by the familiar arithmetic problem, by checking paired lists of numbers to see which are alike and which are different, or by interpreting charts and graphs. In the latter test, a graph may be printed in the test booklet which you are asked to use as the basis for answering questions.

4) Observation

A popular test for law-enforcement positions is the observation test. A picture is shown to you for several minutes, then taken away. Questions about the picture test your ability to observe both details and larger elements.

5) Following directions

In many positions in the public service, the employee must be able to carry out written instructions dependably and accurately. You may be given a chart with several columns, each column listing a variety of information. The questions require you to carry out directions involving the information given in the chart.

6) Skills and aptitudes

Performance tests effectively measure some manual skills and aptitudes. When the skill is one in which you are trained, such as typing or shorthand, you can practice. These tests are often very much like those given in business school or high school courses. For many of the other skills and aptitudes, however, no short-time preparation can be made. Skills and abilities natural to you or that you have developed throughout your lifetime are being tested.

Many of the general questions just described provide all the data needed to answer the questions and ask you to use your reasoning ability to find the answers. Your best preparation for these tests, as well as for tests of facts and ideas, is to be at your physical and mental best. You, no doubt, have your own methods of getting into an exam-taking mood and keeping "in shape." The next section lists some ideas on this subject.

IV. KINDS OF QUESTIONS

Only rarely is the "essay" question, which you answer in narrative form, used in civil service tests. Civil service tests are usually of the short-answer type. Full instructions for answering these questions will be given to you at the examination. But in case this is your first experience with short-answer questions and separate answer sheets, here is what you need to know:

1) Multiple-choice Questions

Most popular of the short-answer questions is the "multiple choice" or "best answer" question. It can be used, for example, to test for factual knowledge, ability to solve problems or judgment in meeting situations found at work.

A multiple-choice question is normally one of three types—

- It can begin with an incomplete statement followed by several possible endings. You are to find the one ending which *best* completes the statement, although some of the others may not be entirely wrong.
- It can also be a complete statement in the form of a question which is answered by choosing one of the statements listed.
- It can be in the form of a problem – again you select the best answer.

Here is an example of a multiple-choice question with a discussion which should give you some clues as to the method for choosing the right answer:

When an employee has a complaint about his assignment, the action which will *best* help him overcome his difficulty is to
- A. discuss his difficulty with his coworkers
- B. take the problem to the head of the organization
- C. take the problem to the person who gave him the assignment
- D. say nothing to anyone about his complaint

In answering this question, you should study each of the choices to find which is best. Consider choice "A" – Certainly an employee may discuss his complaint with fellow employees, but no change or improvement can result, and the complaint remains unresolved. Choice "B" is a poor choice since the head of the organization probably does not know what assignment you have been given, and taking your problem to him is known as "going over the head" of the supervisor. The supervisor, or person who made the assignment, is the person who can clarify it or correct any injustice. Choice "C" is, therefore, correct. To say nothing, as in choice "D," is unwise. Supervisors have and interest in knowing the problems employees are facing, and the employee is seeking a solution to his problem.

2) True/False Questions

The "true/false" or "right/wrong" form of question is sometimes used. Here a complete statement is given. Your job is to decide whether the statement is right or wrong.

SAMPLE: A person-to-person long-distance telephone call costs less than a station-to-station call to the same city.

This statement is wrong, or false, since person-to-person calls are more expensive.

This is not a complete list of all possible question forms, although most of the others are variations of these common types. You will always get complete directions for answering questions. Be sure you understand *how* to mark your answers – ask questions until you do.

V. RECORDING YOUR ANSWERS

For an examination with very few applicants, you may be told to record your answers in the test booklet itself. Separate answer sheets are much more common. If this separate answer sheet is to be scored by machine – and this is often the case – it is highly important that you mark your answers correctly in order to get credit.

An electric scoring machine is often used in civil service offices because of the speed with which papers can be scored. Machine-scored answer sheets must be marked with a pencil, which will be given to you. This pencil has a high graphite content which responds to the electric scoring machine. As a matter of fact, stray dots may register as answers, so do not let your pencil rest on the answer sheet while you are pondering the correct answer. Also, if your pencil lead breaks or is otherwise defective, ask for another.

Since the answer sheet will be dropped in a slot in the scoring machine, be careful not to bend the corners or get the paper crumpled.

The answer sheet normally has five vertical columns of numbers, with 30 numbers to a column. These numbers correspond to the question numbers in your test booklet. After each number, going across the page are four or five pairs of dotted lines. These short dotted lines have small letters or numbers above them. The first two pairs may also have a "T" or "F" above the letters. This indicates that the first two pairs only are to be used if the questions are of the true-false type. If the questions are multiple choice, disregard the "T" and "F" and pay attention only to the small letters or numbers.

Answer your questions in the manner of the sample that follows:

32. The largest city in the United States is
    A. Washington, D.C.
    B. New York City
    C. Chicago
    D. Detroit
    E. San Francisco

1) Choose the answer you think is best. (New York City is the largest, so "B" is correct.)
2) Find the row of dotted lines numbered the same as the question you are answering. (Find row number 32)
3) Find the pair of dotted lines corresponding to the answer. (Find the pair of lines under the mark "B.")
4) Make a solid black mark between the dotted lines.

VI. BEFORE THE TEST

Common sense will help you find procedures to follow to get ready for an examination. Too many of us, however, overlook these sensible measures. Indeed, nervousness and fatigue have been found to be the most serious reasons why applicants fail to do their best on civil service tests. Here is a list of reminders:

- Begin your preparation early – Don't wait until the last minute to go scurrying around for books and materials or to find out what the position is all about.
- Prepare continuously – An hour a night for a week is better than an all-night cram session. This has been definitely established. What is more, a night a

week for a month will return better dividends than crowding your study into a shorter period of time.

- Locate the place of the exam – You have been sent a notice telling you when and where to report for the examination. If the location is in a different town or otherwise unfamiliar to you, it would be well to inquire the best route and learn something about the building.
- Relax the night before the test – Allow your mind to rest. Do not study at all that night. Plan some mild recreation or diversion; then go to bed early and get a good night's sleep.
- Get up early enough to make a leisurely trip to the place for the test – This way unforeseen events, traffic snarls, unfamiliar buildings, etc. will not upset you.
- Dress comfortably – A written test is not a fashion show. You will be known by number and not by name, so wear something comfortable.
- Leave excess paraphernalia at home – Shopping bags and odd bundles will get in your way. You need bring only the items mentioned in the official notice you received; usually everything you need is provided. Do not bring reference books to the exam. They will only confuse those last minutes and be taken away from you when in the test room.
- Arrive somewhat ahead of time – If because of transportation schedules you must get there very early, bring a newspaper or magazine to take your mind off yourself while waiting.
- Locate the examination room – When you have found the proper room, you will be directed to the seat or part of the room where you will sit. Sometimes you are given a sheet of instructions to read while you are waiting. Do not fill out any forms until you are told to do so; just read them and be prepared.
- Relax and prepare to listen to the instructions
- If you have any physical problem that may keep you from doing your best, be sure to tell the test administrator. If you are sick or in poor health, you really cannot do your best on the exam. You can come back and take the test some other time.

VII. AT THE TEST

The day of the test is here and you have the test booklet in your hand. The temptation to get going is very strong. Caution! There is more to success than knowing the right answers. You must know how to identify your papers and understand variations in the type of short-answer question used in this particular examination. Follow these suggestions for maximum results from your efforts:

1) Cooperate with the monitor

The test administrator has a duty to create a situation in which you can be as much at ease as possible. He will give instructions, tell you when to begin, check to see that you are marking your answer sheet correctly, and so on. He is not there to guard you, although he will see that your competitors do not take unfair advantage. He wants to help you do your best.

2) Listen to all instructions

Don't jump the gun! Wait until you understand all directions. In most civil service tests you get more time than you need to answer the questions. So don't be in a hurry.

Read each word of instructions until you clearly understand the meaning. Study the examples, listen to all announcements and follow directions. Ask questions if you do not understand what to do.

3) Identify your papers

Civil service exams are usually identified by number only. You will be assigned a number; you must not put your name on your test papers. Be sure to copy your number correctly. Since more than one exam may be given, copy your exact examination title.

4) Plan your time

Unless you are told that a test is a "speed" or "rate of work" test, speed itself is usually not important. Time enough to answer all the questions will be provided, but this does not mean that you have all day. An overall time limit has been set. Divide the total time (in minutes) by the number of questions to determine the approximate time you have for each question.

5) Do not linger over difficult questions

If you come across a difficult question, mark it with a paper clip (useful to have along) and come back to it when you have been through the booklet. One caution if you do this – be sure to skip a number on your answer sheet as well. Check often to be sure that you have not lost your place and that you are marking in the row numbered the same as the question you are answering.

6) Read the questions

Be sure you know what the question asks! Many capable people are unsuccessful because they failed to *read* the questions correctly.

7) Answer all questions

Unless you have been instructed that a penalty will be deducted for incorrect answers, it is better to guess than to omit a question.

8) Speed tests

It is often better NOT to guess on speed tests. It has been found that on timed tests people are tempted to spend the last few seconds before time is called in marking answers at random – without even reading them – in the hope of picking up a few extra points. To discourage this practice, the instructions may warn you that your score will be "corrected" for guessing. That is, a penalty will be applied. The incorrect answers will be deducted from the correct ones, or some other penalty formula will be used.

9) Review your answers

If you finish before time is called, go back to the questions you guessed or omitted to give them further thought. Review other answers if you have time.

10) Return your test materials

If you are ready to leave before others have finished or time is called, take ALL your materials to the monitor and leave quietly. Never take any test material with you. The monitor can discover whose papers are not complete, and taking a test booklet may be grounds for disqualification.

VIII. EXAMINATION TECHNIQUES

1) Read the general instructions carefully. These are usually printed on the first page of the exam booklet. As a rule, these instructions refer to the timing of the examination; the fact that you should not start work until the signal and must stop work at a signal, etc. If there are any *special* instructions, such as a choice of questions to be answered, make sure that you note this instruction carefully.

2) When you are ready to start work on the examination, that is as soon as the signal has been given, read the instructions to each question booklet, underline any key words or phrases, such as *least, best, outline, describe* and the like. In this way you will tend to answer as requested rather than discover on reviewing your paper that you *listed without describing*, that you selected the *worst* choice rather than the *best* choice, etc.

3) If the examination is of the objective or multiple-choice type – that is, each question will also give a series of possible answers: A, B, C or D, and you are called upon to select the best answer and write the letter next to that answer on your answer paper – it is advisable to start answering each question in turn. There may be anywhere from 50 to 100 such questions in the three or four hours allotted and you can see how much time would be taken if you read through all the questions before beginning to answer any. Furthermore, if you come across a question or group of questions which you know would be difficult to answer, it would undoubtedly affect your handling of all the other questions.

4) If the examination is of the essay type and contains but a few questions, it is a moot point as to whether you should read all the questions before starting to answer any one. Of course, if you are given a choice – say five out of seven and the like – then it is essential to read all the questions so you can eliminate the two that are most difficult. If, however, you are asked to answer all the questions, there may be danger in trying to answer the easiest one first because you may find that you will spend too much time on it. The best technique is to answer the first question, then proceed to the second, etc.

5) Time your answers. Before the exam begins, write down the time it started, then add the time allowed for the examination and write down the time it must be completed, then divide the time available somewhat as follows:
   - If 3-1/2 hours are allowed, that would be 210 minutes. If you have 80 objective-type questions, that would be an average of 2-1/2 minutes per question. Allow yourself no more than 2 minutes per question, or a total of 160 minutes, which will permit about 50 minutes to review.
   - If for the time allotment of 210 minutes there are 7 essay questions to answer, that would average about 30 minutes a question. Give yourself only 25 minutes per question so that you have about 35 minutes to review.

6) The most important instruction is to *read each question* and make sure you know what is wanted. The second most important instruction is to *time yourself properly* so that you answer every question. The third most

important instruction is to *answer every question.* Guess if you have to but include something for each question. Remember that you will receive no credit for a blank and will probably receive some credit if you write something in answer to an essay question. If you guess a letter – say "B" for a multiple-choice question – you may have guessed right. If you leave a blank as an answer to a multiple-choice question, the examiners may respect your feelings but it will not add a point to your score. Some exams may penalize you for wrong answers, so in such cases *only*, you may not want to guess unless you have some basis for your answer.

7) Suggestions
   a. Objective-type questions
     1. Examine the question booklet for proper sequence of pages and questions
     2. Read all instructions carefully
     3. Skip any question which seems too difficult; return to it after all other questions have been answered
     4. Apportion your time properly; do not spend too much time on any single question or group of questions
     5. Note and underline key words – *all, most, fewest, least, best, worst, same, opposite,* etc.
     6. Pay particular attention to negatives
     7. Note unusual option, e.g., unduly long, short, complex, different or similar in content to the body of the question
     8. Observe the use of "hedging" words – *probably, may, most likely,* etc.
     9. Make sure that your answer is put next to the same number as the question
     10. Do not second-guess unless you have good reason to believe the second answer is definitely more correct
     11. Cross out original answer if you decide another answer is more accurate; do not erase until you are ready to hand your paper in
     12. Answer all questions; guess unless instructed otherwise
     13. Leave time for review

   b. Essay questions
     1. Read each question carefully
     2. Determine exactly what is wanted. Underline key words or phrases.
     3. Decide on outline or paragraph answer
     4. Include many different points and elements unless asked to develop any one or two points or elements
     5. Show impartiality by giving pros and cons unless directed to select one side only
     6. Make and write down any assumptions you find necessary to answer the questions
     7. Watch your English, grammar, punctuation and choice of words
     8. Time your answers; don't crowd material

8) Answering the essay question

Most essay questions can be answered by framing the specific response around several key words or ideas. Here are a few such key words or ideas:

M's: manpower, materials, methods, money, management

P's: purpose, program, policy, plan, procedure, practice, problems, pitfalls, personnel, public relations

a. Six basic steps in handling problems:

1. Preliminary plan and background development
2. Collect information, data and facts
3. Analyze and interpret information, data and facts
4. Analyze and develop solutions as well as make recommendations
5. Prepare report and sell recommendations
6. Install recommendations and follow up effectiveness

b. Pitfalls to avoid

1. *Taking things for granted* – A statement of the situation does not necessarily imply that each of the elements is necessarily true; for example, a complaint may be invalid and biased so that all that can be taken for granted is that a complaint has been registered

2. *Considering only one side of a situation* – Wherever possible, indicate several alternatives and then point out the reasons you selected the best one

3. *Failing to indicate follow up* – Whenever your answer indicates action on your part, make certain that you will take proper follow-up action to see how successful your recommendations, procedures or actions turn out to be

4. *Taking too long in answering any single question* – Remember to time your answers properly

IX. AFTER THE TEST

Scoring procedures differ in detail among civil service jurisdictions although the general principles are the same. Whether the papers are hand-scored or graded by machine we have described, they are nearly always graded by number. That is, the person who marks the paper knows only the number – never the name – of the applicant. Not until all the papers have been graded will they be matched with names. If other tests, such as training and experience or oral interview ratings have been given, scores will be combined. Different parts of the examination usually have different weights. For example, the written test might count 60 percent of the final grade, and a rating of training and experience 40 percent. In many jurisdictions, veterans will have a certain number of points added to their grades.

After the final grade has been determined, the names are placed in grade order and an eligible list is established. There are various methods for resolving ties between those who get the same final grade – probably the most common is to place first the name of the person whose application was received first. Job offers are made from the eligible list in the order the names appear on it. You will be notified of your grade and your rank as soon as all these computations have been made. This will be done as rapidly as possible.

People who are found to meet the requirements in the announcement are called "eligibles." Their names are put on a list of eligible candidates. An eligible's chances of getting a job depend on how high he stands on this list and how fast agencies are filling jobs from the list.

When a job is to be filled from a list of eligibles, the agency asks for the names of people on the list of eligibles for that job. When the civil service commission receives this request, it sends to the agency the names of the three people highest on this list. Or, if the job to be filled has specialized requirements, the office sends the agency the names of the top three persons who meet these requirements from the general list.

The appointing officer makes a choice from among the three people whose names were sent to him. If the selected person accepts the appointment, the names of the others are put back on the list to be considered for future openings.

That is the rule in hiring from all kinds of eligible lists, whether they are for typist, carpenter, chemist, or something else. For every vacancy, the appointing officer has his choice of any one of the top three eligibles on the list. This explains why the person whose name is on top of the list sometimes does not get an appointment when some of the persons lower on the list do. If the appointing officer chooses the second or third eligible, the No. 1 eligible does not get a job at once, but stays on the list until he is appointed or the list is terminated.

X. HOW TO PASS THE INTERVIEW TEST

The examination for which you applied requires an oral interview test. You have already taken the written test and you are now being called for the interview test – the final part of the formal examination.

You may think that it is not possible to prepare for an interview test and that there are no procedures to follow during an interview. Our purpose is to point out some things you can do in advance that will help you and some good rules to follow and pitfalls to avoid while you are being interviewed.

What is an interview supposed to test?

The written examination is designed to test the technical knowledge and competence of the candidate; the oral is designed to evaluate intangible qualities, not readily measured otherwise, and to establish a list showing the relative fitness of each candidate – as measured against his competitors – for the position sought. Scoring is not on the basis of "right" and "wrong," but on a sliding scale of values ranging from "not passable" to "outstanding." As a matter of fact, it is possible to achieve a relatively low score without a single "incorrect" answer because of evident weakness in the qualities being measured.

Occasionally, an examination may consist entirely of an oral test – either an individual or a group oral. In such cases, information is sought concerning the technical knowledges and abilities of the candidate, since there has been no written examination for this purpose. More commonly, however, an oral test is used to supplement a written examination.

Who conducts interviews?

The composition of oral boards varies among different jurisdictions. In nearly all, a representative of the personnel department serves as chairman. One of the members of the board may be a representative of the department in which the candidate would work. In some cases, "outside experts" are used, and, frequently, a businessman or some other representative of the general public is asked to serve. Labor and management or other special groups may be represented. The aim is to secure the services of experts in the appropriate field.

However the board is composed, it is a good idea (and not at all improper or unethical) to ascertain in advance of the interview who the members are and what groups they represent. When you are introduced to them, you will have some idea of their backgrounds and interests, and at least you will not stutter and stammer over their names.

What should be done before the interview?

While knowledge about the board members is useful and takes some of the surprise element out of the interview, there is other preparation which is more substantive. It *is* possible to prepare for an oral interview – in several ways:

1) Keep a copy of your application and review it carefully before the interview

This may be the only document before the oral board, and the starting point of the interview. Know what education and experience you have listed there, and the sequence and dates of all of it. Sometimes the board will ask you to review the highlights of your experience for them; you should not have to hem and haw doing it.

2) Study the class specification and the examination announcement

Usually, the oral board has one or both of these to guide them. The qualities, characteristics or knowledges required by the position sought are stated in these documents. They offer valuable clues as to the nature of the oral interview. For example, if the job involves supervisory responsibilities, the announcement will usually indicate that knowledge of modern supervisory methods and the qualifications of the candidate as a supervisor will be tested. If so, you can expect such questions, frequently in the form of a hypothetical situation which you are expected to solve. NEVER go into an oral without knowledge of the duties and responsibilities of the job you seek.

3) Think through each qualification required

Try to visualize the kind of questions you would ask if you were a board member. How well could you answer them? Try especially to appraise your own knowledge and background in each area, *measured against the job sought*, and identify any areas in which you are weak. Be critical and realistic – do not flatter yourself.

4) Do some general reading in areas in which you feel you may be weak

For example, if the job involves supervision and your past experience has NOT, some general reading in supervisory methods and practices, particularly in the field of human relations, might be useful. Do NOT study agency procedures or detailed manuals. The oral board will be testing your understanding and capacity, not your memory.

5) Get a good night's sleep and watch your general health and mental attitude

You will want a clear head at the interview. Take care of a cold or any other minor ailment, and of course, no hangovers.

What should be done on the day of the interview?

Now comes the day of the interview itself. Give yourself plenty of time to get there. Plan to arrive somewhat ahead of the scheduled time, particularly if your appointment is in the fore part of the day. If a previous candidate fails to appear, the board might be ready for you a bit early. By early afternoon an oral board is almost invariably behind schedule if there are many candidates, and you may have to wait.

Take along a book or magazine to read, or your application to review, but leave any extraneous material in the waiting room when you go in for your interview. In any event, relax and compose yourself.

The matter of dress is important. The board is forming impressions about you – from your experience, your manners, your attitude, and your appearance. Give your personal appearance careful attention. Dress your best, but not your flashiest. Choose conservative, appropriate clothing, and be sure it is immaculate. This is a business interview, and your appearance should indicate that you regard it as such. Besides, being well groomed and properly dressed will help boost your confidence.

Sooner or later, someone will call your name and escort you into the interview room. *This is it.* From here on you are on your own. It is too late for any more preparation. But remember, you asked for this opportunity to prove your fitness, and you are here because your request was granted.

What happens when you go in?

The usual sequence of events will be as follows: The clerk (who is often the board stenographer) will introduce you to the chairman of the oral board, who will introduce you to the other members of the board. Acknowledge the introductions before you sit down. Do not be surprised if you find a microphone facing you or a stenotypist sitting by. Oral interviews are usually recorded in the event of an appeal or other review.

Usually the chairman of the board will open the interview by reviewing the highlights of your education and work experience from your application – primarily for the benefit of the other members of the board, as well as to get the material into the record. Do not interrupt or comment unless there is an error or significant misinterpretation; if that is the case, do not hesitate. But do not quibble about insignificant matters. Also, he will usually ask you some question about your education, experience or your present job – partly to get you to start talking and to establish the interviewing "rapport." He may start the actual questioning, or turn it over to one of the other members. Frequently, each member undertakes the questioning on a particular area, one in which he is perhaps most competent, so you can expect each member to participate in the examination. Because time is limited, you may also expect some rather abrupt switches in the direction the questioning takes, so do not be upset by it. Normally, a board member will not pursue a single line of questioning unless he discovers a particular strength or weakness.

After each member has participated, the chairman will usually ask whether any member has any further questions, then will ask you if you have anything you wish to add. Unless you are expecting this question, it may floor you. Worse, it may start you off on an extended, extemporaneous speech. The board is not usually seeking more information. The question is principally to offer you a last opportunity to present further qualifications or to indicate that you have nothing to add. So, if you feel that a significant qualification or characteristic has been overlooked, it is proper to point it out in a sentence or so. Do not compliment the board on the thoroughness of their examination – they have been sketchy, and you know it. If you wish, merely say, "No thank you, I have nothing further to add." This is a point where you can "talk yourself out" of a good impression or fail to present an important bit of information. Remember, *you close the interview yourself.*

The chairman will then say, "That is all, Mr. _____, thank you." Do not be startled; the interview is over, and quicker than you think. Thank him, gather your belongings and take your leave. Save your sigh of relief for the other side of the door.

How to put your best foot forward

Throughout this entire process, you may feel that the board individually and collectively is trying to pierce your defenses, seek out your hidden weaknesses and embarrass and confuse you. Actually, this is not true. They are obliged to make an appraisal of your qualifications for the job you are seeking, and they want to see you in your best light. Remember, they must interview all candidates and a non-cooperative candidate may become a failure in spite of their best efforts to bring out his qualifications. Here are 15 suggestions that will help you:

1) Be natural – Keep your attitude confident, not cocky

If you are not confident that you can do the job, do not expect the board to be. Do not apologize for your weaknesses, try to bring out your strong points. The board is interested in a positive, not negative, presentation. Cockiness will antagonize any board member and make him wonder if you are covering up a weakness by a false show of strength.

2) Get comfortable, but don't lounge or sprawl

Sit erectly but not stiffly. A careless posture may lead the board to conclude that you are careless in other things, or at least that you are not impressed by the importance of the occasion. Either conclusion is natural, even if incorrect. Do not fuss with your clothing, a pencil or an ashtray. Your hands may occasionally be useful to emphasize a point; do not let them become a point of distraction.

3) Do not wisecrack or make small talk

This is a serious situation, and your attitude should show that you consider it as such. Further, the time of the board is limited – they do not want to waste it, and neither should you.

4) Do not exaggerate your experience or abilities

In the first place, from information in the application or other interviews and sources, the board may know more about you than you think. Secondly, you probably will not get away with it. An experienced board is rather adept at spotting such a situation, so do not take the chance.

5) If you know a board member, do not make a point of it, yet do not hide it

Certainly you are not fooling him, and probably not the other members of the board. Do not try to take advantage of your acquaintanceship – it will probably do you little good.

6) Do not dominate the interview

Let the board do that. They will give you the clues – do not assume that you have to do all the talking. Realize that the board has a number of questions to ask you, and do not try to take up all the interview time by showing off your extensive knowledge of the answer to the first one.

7) Be attentive

You only have 20 minutes or so, and you should keep your attention at its sharpest throughout. When a member is addressing a problem or question to you, give him your undivided attention. Address your reply principally to him, but do not exclude the other board members.

8) Do not interrupt

A board member may be stating a problem for you to analyze. He will ask you a question when the time comes. Let him state the problem, and wait for the question.

9) Make sure you understand the question

Do not try to answer until you are sure what the question is. If it is not clear, restate it in your own words or ask the board member to clarify it for you. However, do not haggle about minor elements.

10) Reply promptly but not hastily

A common entry on oral board rating sheets is "candidate responded readily," or "candidate hesitated in replies." Respond as promptly and quickly as you can, but do not jump to a hasty, ill-considered answer.

11) Do not be peremptory in your answers

A brief answer is proper – but do not fire your answer back. That is a losing game from your point of view. The board member can probably ask questions much faster than you can answer them.

12) Do not try to create the answer you think the board member wants

He is interested in what kind of mind you have and how it works – not in playing games. Furthermore, he can usually spot this practice and will actually grade you down on it.

13) Do not switch sides in your reply merely to agree with a board member

Frequently, a member will take a contrary position merely to draw you out and to see if you are willing and able to defend your point of view. Do not start a debate, yet do not surrender a good position. If a position is worth taking, it is worth defending.

14) Do not be afraid to admit an error in judgment if you are shown to be wrong

The board knows that you are forced to reply without any opportunity for careful consideration. Your answer may be demonstrably wrong. If so, admit it and get on with the interview.

15) Do not dwell at length on your present job

The opening question may relate to your present assignment. Answer the question but do not go into an extended discussion. You are being examined for a *new* job, not your present one. As a matter of fact, try to phrase ALL your answers in terms of the job for which you are being examined.

Basis of Rating

Probably you will forget most of these "do's" and "don'ts" when you walk into the oral interview room. Even remembering them all will not ensure you a passing grade. Perhaps you did not have the qualifications in the first place. But remembering them will help you to put your best foot forward, without treading on the toes of the board members.

Rumor and popular opinion to the contrary notwithstanding, an oral board wants you to make the best appearance possible. They know you are under pressure – but they also want to see how you respond to it as a guide to what your reaction would be under the pressures of the job you seek. They will be influenced by the degree of poise you display, the personal traits you show and the manner in which you respond.

EXAMINATION SECTION

EXAMINATION SECTION
TEST 1

DIRECTIONS: Each question or incomplete statement is followed by several suggested
answers or completions. Select the one that BEST answers the question or
completes the statement. *PRINT THE LETTER OF THE CORRECT ANSWER
IN THE SPACE AT THE RIGHT.*

1.   Of the following, the size of hard coal which is the SMALLEST is   1._____

    A.   egg   B.   stove   C.   broken   D.   buckwheat

2.   If the CO_2 content of the flue gases of an oil burner is very high, it USUALLY indicates   2._____

    A.   too much oil admitted to the furnace
    B.   good combustion of fuel
    C.   good circulation of steam
    D.   excessive steam production

3.   When a steam radiator in a one-pipe gravity system is air-bound, the cause is *most likely*   3._____
to be

    A.   defective air valve
    B.   air entering through a leaking line
    C.   insufficient steam pressure
    D.   defective gate valve

4.   Of the following, the one which is *most unlikely* to cause warping or burning of grate bars   4._____
is

    A.   leaving grates uneven after shaking
    B.   allowing free passage of air through the bars
    C.   accumulating ashes in the ashpit
    D.   shaking all ashes through to the ashpit in an active furnace

5.   A wet return is BEST defined as a   5._____

    A.   return line below the level of water in the boiler
    B.   return that contains water as well as steam
    C.   return that has an improper pitch causing backing up of water
    D.   gravity return from which air has been removed

6.   The MAIN supply of air for the burning of fuel in a coal-fired boiler enters through the   6._____
_____ damper.

    A.   fire door   B.   ashpit door
    C.   breeching   D.   check

7.   Steam traps are devices which serve to   7._____

    A.   by-pass steam flow where radiators are filled with steam
    B.   shut down rate of steam flow when steam temperature is too high
    C.   separate air and condensate from steam in steam heating systems
    D.   prevent the development of high steam pressures by releasing excess steam

8. When the diaphragm or bellows of a thermostatic radiator trap is found to be dirty, it is USUALLY cleaned with   8.___

   A. kerosene
                  B. carbon tetrachloride
   C. mild soap and water
        D. turpentine

9. It is found that water is being carried over from an operating boiler into the steam main. Of the following, the one that is LEAST likely as the possible cause is   9.___

   A. water level higher than specified for the boiler
   B. grease and dirt in the boiler
   C. excessive rate of output
   D. insufficient installed radiation

10. Of the following, the PROPER step to take when firing a boiler by the coking method is to   10.___

   A. push the live coals to the rear of the grates and add fresh coal to the front part of the grates
   B. spread out the live coals and cover them frequently with a thin layer of fresh coal
   C. push the live coals to one side and place fresh coals on the other side, changing sides each time coal is added
   D. shovel the fresh coal on the rear of the grates and then cover them partly with live coals

11. Turpentine is added to paint MAINLY to   11.___

   A. enable it to dry more rapidly
   B. dissolve the pigment in the paint
   C. add corrosion resisting properties to the paint
   D. thin out the paint

12. Automatic operation of a sump pump is controlled by the   12.___

   A. electric switch
              B. float
   C. foot valve
              D. centrifugal driving unit

13. Kerosene costs 36 cents a quart. At that rate, two gallons would cost   13.___

   A. $1.44
       B. $2.16
       C. $2.88
       D. $3.60

14. A PROPER procedure in the event of fire in a school building is to   14.___

   A. shut down all utilities - gas, electricity, and water
   B. maintain normal steam pressure in high pressure boilers equipped with auxiliaries driven by utility company electric power
   C. shut down all ventilating fans on central duct systems
   D. open all fire doors on the various floors to ventilate the fire

15. Piping used to carry electric wiring is COMMONLY called   15.___

   A. conduit
       B. leader
       C. conductor
       D. sleeve

16. The MAIN objection to using a copper penny in place of a blown fuse is that   16.___

   A. the penny will conduct electric current
   B. the penny will reduce the current flowing in the line
   C. melting of the penny will probably occur
   D. the line will not be protected against excessive current

17. A rip saw is GENERALLY used to cut   17.____

    A. corners
    B. uneven ragged lumber strips
    C. with the grain
    D. across the grain

18. Sweating USUALLY occurs in pipes that   18.____

    A. contain hot water
    B. contain cold water
    C. are chrome plated
    D. require insulation

19. Workmen's Compensation insurance USUALLY provides   19.____

    A. employee benefits whether or not the injury was his fault
    B. employee benefits only if the employee was not negligent or exceptionally careless
    C. medical benefits in all cases, and compensation if no negligence or deliberate injury is found
    D. all benefits if absent from work four days or more

20. Of the following, the MOST important reason for making supply inventories is to   20.____

    A. schedule work assignments properly
    B. make certain that the supply room is in an orderly condition
    C. determine if employees are working efficiently
    D. check on the use of materials

21. Suppose that you are preparing a semi-annual requisition for janitorial supplies. The PROPER procedure in preparing the requisition is to   21.____

    A. order one and one-half times the amount actually needed to be sure of an adequate reserve
    B. order the amount actually needed as based on past use and probable needs
    C. ask each member of your staff to submit a statement of the supplies he will need for the next six months
    D. order 10% more than the previous year to cover all possible emergencies

22. Beginning of period   22.____

End of period

The amount of gas in cubic feet used during the measured period is
A. 183   B. 283   C. 362   D. 454

23. The MOST probable cause of foaming of a boiler that has been recently installed is   23.__

    A. poor draft
    B. higher than normal water level
    C. grease and oil in boiler
    D. excessive rate of output

24. When banking a fire, a PROPER step to take is to   24.__

    A. avoid any bright spots in the fuel bed
    B. close damper tightly
    C. open ashpit doors fully
    D. close fire doors

25. Of the following, the one which is considered poor practice in boiler operation is keeping   25.__

    A. valves at the top and bottom of the water gauge glass open whenever operating boiler
    B. steam gauge cock open at all times when boiler is in operation
    C. fuel bed as light and shallow as possible to maintain fuel economy
    D. a thin ash layer over the grate to protect the bars from heat

26. A PROPER procedure in boiler operation is to blow down   26.__

    A. boilers and condensate tanks weekly
    B. the water column daily
    C. the water column weekly
    D. boilers only when necessary

27. The MAIN purpose of a condensate pump is to   27.__

    A. return water from the return lines to a boiler
    B. pump make-up water to maintain water level
    C. maintain steam pressure in the supply lines
    D. provide for continuous draining of radiators under pressure

28. In an oil-fired plant, the emergency or remote control switch is USUALLY located   28.__

    A. at the entrance to the boiler room
    B. next to the oil burner
    C. at the panel board in the boiler room
    D. at the electrical distribution panel for the building

29. A safety device which is COMMONLY used in oil burner operation to detect flame failure and shut down the burner is a   29.__

    A. thermostat   B. stackswitch
    C. aquastat   D. yulatrol

30. Of the following items, the one that has LEAST relation to the ignition system of an auto-   30.____
    matic horizontal rotary cup oil burner is a

    A. transformer   B. electrode
    C. gas valve   D. oil metering valve

31. The pressure of oil in the oil supply piping to a rotary cup oil burner is about 40 pounds.   31.____
    This pressure is maintained MAINLY in order to

    A. bring the oil into the atomizing cup
    B. mix the oil together with the primary air
    C. operate the magnetic oil valve
    D. avoid having the oil spray strike the edge of the oil nozzle

32. The atomizing cup of an oil burner shows carbon deposits. Of the following, the MOST   32.____
    desirable way to remove these deposits is to

    A. use a scraper, followed by light rubbing with 00 sandpaper
    B. wash the cup and nozzle with a mild trisodium phosphate solution and dry with a
        cloth
    C. use kerosene to loosen the deposits and wipe with a soft cloth
    D. apply a hot flame to the carbonized surfaces to burn off the carbon deposits

33. The MAJOR purpose of keeping the boiler filled with water during the non-heating sea-   33.____
    son is that

    A. corrosion of interior parts will be prevented
    B. leaks in the boiler or piping will be detected more easily before the heating season
        begins
    C. no time will be lost in filling the boiler when the heating season starts
    D. scale deposits and impurities in the water will be reduced to a minimum

34. A MAJOR disadvantage of self-closing faucets in lines operating under moderate water   34.____
    pressure is that they

    A. close too rapidly
    B. frequently produce water hammer
    C. open too easily
    D. tend to become filled with sediment

35. When lamps are wired in parallel, the failure of one lamp will   35.____

    A. break the electric circuit to the other lamps
    B. have no effect on the power supply to the other lamps
    C. increase noticeably the light production of the other lamps
    D. cause excessive current to flow through the other lamps

36. A cotter pin is used to   36.____

    A. set tile
    B. reduce bushings
    C. strengthen bolts to stand a greater pull
    D. keep a nut from working loose

37. Of the following valves, the one which is automatic in operation is   37.___

    A. check   B. globe   C. angle   D. gate

38. The name of a fitting used to make a turn in the direction of a pipe line is   38.___

    A. union   B. bushing   C. elbow   D. coupling

39. If the flush tank of a water-closet fixture overflows, the fault is likely to be   39.___

    A. failure of the ball to seat properly
    B. excessive water pressure
    C. defective trap in the toilet bowl
    D. water-logged float

40. For the purpose of fire prevention, it is MOST important that the custodian   40.___

    A. know how to attack fires whatever their size
    B. detect and eliminate every possible fire hazard
    C. train his staff to place inflammables in fireproof containers
    D. see that halls, corridors, and exits are not blocked

41. In addition to his utilitarian duties and responsibilities, the custodian shall have general   41.___
responsibility to assist the educational system by developing the cultural function of envi-
ronment. This should follow automatically if his utilitarian work is well accomplished. This
statement means *most nearly* that

    A. the custodian must act as a teacher of school children as well as operating and
        maintaining his building in accordance with highest standards
    B. if a custodian observes a teacher neglecting to discipline children properly, it is his
        duty to correct this failure
    C. the custodian must train his staff just as the educational system teaches children
        so that both achieve a higher cultural level
    D. if a custodian operates and maintains his building properly, he will assist in
        enabling teachers to do a better job

42. When you hire a new employee and you are preparing to train him in the work he is to   42.___
perform, the FIRST thing to do is to

    A. tell him what his job is and find out what he already knows about it
    B. prepare a written description of the tasks the employee is to do and have him study
        them
    C. make certain that the employee has all the proper tools and materials and knows
        how to store them
    D. have him work along with another older employee to learn the requirements of the
        job

43. A cleaner tells you that several teachers do not keep their rooms clean, resulting in extra   43.___
work for him. Assuming that he is correct in his claim, the MOST desirable step to take is
to

    A. visit the teachers directly and ask them to manage their classes so as to avoid
        excessive cleaning
    B. suggest to the principal that he discuss this cleaning problem with his teaching
        staff
    C. advise the cleaner to discuss the matter with the teachers involved
    D. tell the cleaner that nothing can be done and that he'll just have to do the extra
        cleaning

44. When a repair is required in your school, the FIRST thing to do is to

    A. determine if you and your staff can handle it
    B. ask for assistance from the repair shop
    C. find out exactly what has to be done
    D. make a list of the materials and tools needed

44.____

45. A teacher complains to you that one of your staff failed to acknowledge his greeting and was not a very pleasant person. The MOST reasonable thing to do is to

    A. tell the teacher that the employee does his work well and that that is all you can ask of him
    B. advise the teacher to speak to the school principal if he has any real grievance
    C. tell the employee to be more polite to the teacher or he may lose his job
    D. discuss with your staff the need for a more friendly attitude toward the teaching staff

45.____

46. A cleaner asks to have his hours of work changed. You find that you cannot grant this request because you require coverage during those hours. Under the circumstances, you should

    A. tell the cleaner that you cannot grant his request because the main office frowns on schedule changes
    B. deny his request and give your reasons for such denial
    C. advise the cleaner that if you changed his hours, other employees might make similar requests
    D. tell the cleaner that he should try to find another job with hours suitable to his needs

46.____

47. The purpose of a safety valve on a steam boiler is to

    A. start the feed pump when the water is low
    B. dampen the fire when the boiler is overheated
    C. shut off the feed pump when enough water is let into the boiler
    D. release the steam when the pressure gets too great

47.____

48. A device which is LEAST likely to be found in low pressure heating plants is a(n)

    A. vacuum pump   B. inverted bucket trap
    C. economizer   D. Hartford return connection

48.____

49. Baffle plates are sometimes put into furnaces to

    A. change the direction of heated gases
    B. increase the combustion of the fuel
    C. retard the burning of the gases
    D. prevent overloading of the combustion chamber

49.____

50.   An operating boiler explosion may be caused by

    A.   accumulation of gas in the furnace
    B.   too deep a fire
    C.   overpressure of steam
    D.   too much water in the boiler

_____

KEY (CORRECT ANSWERS)

1. D	11. D	21. B	31. A	41. D
2. B	12. B	22. C	32. C	42. A
3. A	13. C	23. C	33. A	43. B
4. B	14. C	24. D	34. B	44. C
5. A	15. A	25. C	35. B	45. D
6. B	16. D	26. B	36. D	46. B
7. C	17. C	27. A	37. A	47. D
8. A	18. B	28. A	38. C	48. C
9. D	19. A	29. B	39. D	49. A
10. A	20. D	30. D	40. B	50. C

_____

TEST 2

DIRECTIONS: Each question consists of a statement. You are to indicate whether the statement is TRUE (T) or FALSE (F). *PRINT THE LETTER OF THE CORRECT ANSWER IN THE SPACE AT THE RIGHT.*

1. The amount of furniture in a classroom determines to a large extent the time that will be required to sweep it.

    1.____

2. Exterior bronze should be wiped periodically with a soft cloth dampened with a light oil such as lemon oil

    2.____

3. A gallon of kerosene is heavier than a gallon of water.

    3.____

4. The purpose of boiler feedwater treatment compound added to boiler water is to eliminate minor leaks in the boiler shell.

    4.____

5. Air pockets occur more frequently in one-pipe heating systems than in two-pipe systems.

    5.____

6. Floor brushes should always be hung on pegs when not in use.

    6.____

7. A floor brush, when used on a classroom floor, will stir up more dust than a good corn broom.

    7.____

8. When sweeping a classroom with fixed desks and seats, the cleaner should use push strokes rather than pull strokes whenever possible.

    8.____

9. Stick shellac is often used to fill in scratches and dents in furniture.

    9.____

10. Although an ammonia solution is a good glass cleanser, it may darken the putty or painted frames of windows.

    10.____

11. Chamois skins should be completely dry if they are to be used to dry windows or exterior glass.

    11.____

12. The portable vacuum cleaner used in a school can be applied effectively to remove soot from boiler tubes.

    12.____

13. If classroom floors are cleaned by means of a heavy-duty vacuum cleaner, they need not be cleaned daily.

    13.____

14. Calcimined ceilings should be washed with lukewarm water occasionally to remove the accumulated dirt.

    14.____

15. Corn brooms should be wet with warm water once or twice a week to keep the fibers flexible.

    15.____

16. A good time to wash windows is when the sun is shining on them.

    16.____

17. When a floor is to be mopped, the cleaner should plan to mop only small areas at a time.

    17.____

18. When mopping, the mop stroke used should be wide enough so that the mop can touch the baseboards of the room.

    18.____

19. Toilet room odors tend to become more noticeable as the temperature of the room goes down.   19.___

20. Sweeping of a toilet floor should usually start at the door entrance and end at the far corner of the room.   20.___

21. When a mopping job is finished, the floor should be practically dry.   21.___

22. Dirt should be cleaned out from behind radiators before a classroom or corridor is swept.   22.___

23. When grease is to be dissolved in a clogged drain, it is more desirable to use lye than caustic potash.   23.___

24. A purpose for which school classroom floors are oiled is to help preserve the wood.   24.___

25. It usually takes less time to sweep an oiled wood floor than an unoiled wood floor.   25.___

26. It is a good idea to soak new mop heads in boiling hot water for a short time before using them.   26.___

27. A desirable way to remove dry paint from glass is to use a very fine sandpaper.   27.___

28. A nail comb is commonly used to clean grease and dirt from the surfaces of nails.   28.___

29. A force cup or *plumbers friend* is used to remove obstructions in plumbing fixtures.   29.___

30. Panic bolts are usually found attached to swing-type window frames.   30.___

31. Good conductors of heat make good insulating material for covering hot water piping.   31.___

32. Slate blackboards in classrooms should usually be washed once a week.   32.___

33. A soda-acid fire extinguisher must be recharged after each use, no matter how slightly it has been used.   33.___

34. It is not practical to varnish wood floors in schools because the varnish coat is soon marred by heavy traffic.   34.___

35. A circular motion in washing and drying window glass is a more rapid and efficient method than a back-and-forth method.   35.___

36. The highest number visible on a steam gauge indicates the maximum allowable pressure in the boiler.   36.___

37. The outside doors of school buildings should open inward.   37.___

38. For interior building wiring, No. 14 wire is usually thicker than No. 12 wire.   38.___

39. Natural ventilation is obtained by adjusting the openings of windows and transoms.   39.___

40. Floor hair brushes should, in general, be kept dry because water tends to ruin them.   40.___

41. Wood floors should be mopped across the grain wherever possible.   41.___

42. Pails filled with cleaning solutions for mopping a floor should be placed on a wet space to prevent rings.   42._____

43. To effectively clean linoleum floors, very hot water should be used.   43._____

44. Cork tile requires a sealer coat before it is waxed for the first time.   44._____

45. The time it should take to dust the furniture of an average classroom each morning is about 5 or 6 minutes.   45._____

46. High dusting of classrooms should follow dusting of chairs, desks, and window sills.   46._____

47. Flathead screws should be countersunk into the material fastened.   47._____

48. The size of a nut is given by the diameter and number of threads per inch of the bolt it fits.   48._____

49. A good practice in boiler operation is to remove ashes from ashpits once a week during the heating season.   49._____

50. A transformer is a device used to raise or lower A.C. voltage.   50._____

KEY (CORRECT ANSWERS)

1.	T	11.	F	21.	T	31.	F	41.	F
2.	T	12.	T	22.	T	32.	T	42.	T
3.	F	13.	F	23.	F	33.	T	43.	F
4.	F	14.	F	24.	T	34.	T	44.	T
5.	F	15.	T	25.	T	35.	F	45.	T
6.	T	16.	F	26.	T	36.	F	46.	F
7.	F	17.	T	27.	F	37.	F	47.	T
8.	T	18.	F	28.	F	38.	F	48.	T
9.	T	19.	F	29.	T	39.	T	49.	F
10.	T	20.	F	30.	F	40.	T	50.	T

TEST 3

DIRECTIONS: Each question consists of a statement. You are to indicate whether the statement is TRUE (T) or FALSE (F). *PRINT THE LETTER OF THE CORRECT ANSWER IN THE SPACE AT THE RIGHT.*

1. White spots on waxed woodwork due to water or dampness may be removed with alcohol.   1.___

2. A counter brush should not be used to sweep under radiators or lockers.   2.___

3. A good way to dispose of waste paper in a school building is to burn the paper in the steam heating furnace.   3.___

4. Oxalic acid can be used to remove ink stains and rust from woodwork.   4.___

5. A desirable method of removing fingerprints and hardened dirt from porcelain fixtures is to apply a strong coarse powder cleanser.   5.___

6. Wet mop filler replacements are ordered by the weight of the filler, not the length of the strands.   6.___

7. A desirable method of controlling unpleasant odors in a washroom is to use pungent deodorants.   7.___

8. Fuses for branch lighting circuits are usually rated in watts.   8.___

9. The main purpose of oil in a bearing is to prevent the metal parts from touching.   9.___

10. Metal lighting fixtures should not be washed, but should be dusted and wiped lightly with a damp cloth.   10.___

11. The washing of painted walls should begin at the top and proceed down to the bottom of the wall.   11.___

12. Check valves are used to control the direction of flow of water or steam.   12.___

13. A blow-off valve on a boiler is used mainly to reduce steam pressure.   13.___

14. A wood floor should be slightly damp from washing immediately before oil is sprayed on it.   14.___

15. If an oil sprayer nozzle is rusty and gummy, it should be soaked in kerosene for a few days.   15.___

16. Chest x-ray examinations are required for school employees to check on their heart condition.   16.___

17. Auditoriums and assembly rooms usually require brighter lighting than gymnasiums.   17.___

18. The national flag should be displayed on every school day, but not on legal holidays.   18.___

19. The soda-acid fire extinguisher is not affected by freezing temperatures.   19.___

20. Clear cold water should be used to rinse rubber tile floors after they have been mopped. 20.____

21. New asphalt tile floors require the use of a sealer or lacquer to seal the pores. 21.____

22. Soapsuds are often used to locate gas leaks in gas lines. 22.____

23. A kilowatt equals 1000 watts. 23.____

24. The very first step a custodian should take when a water pipe bursts is to call for a plumber. 24.____

25. *Rock Island Sheepswool* is a term usually applied to natural sponges. 25.____

26. There is less danger of electric shock when electric wires are touched with wet hands than with dry hands. 26.____

27. Air for ventilation of school buildings should never be recirculated. 27.____

28. Sweeping compound for use on linoleum and asphalt tile should contain sawdust, floor oil, and water wax. 28.____

29. Chlordane is useful as an insecticide for the control of crawling insects such as roaches. 29.____

30. Soda-acid fire extinguishers for use in school buildings usually have a gallon capacity. 30.____

31. Kick plates of doors should be lubricated about once a month. 31.____

32. A stillson wrench is usually used on heads and nuts of bolts. 32.____

33. No. 000 steel wool is coarser than No. 0 steel wool. 33.____

34. The preferred type of paint for the walls of school classrooms is a durable glossy enamel. 34.____

35. More accidents result from unsafe actions than from unsafe conditions. 35.____

36. The steam gauge cock should always be open when the boiler is operating. 36.____

37. When a wire carrying current becomes hot, it indicates that the fuse in the line has blown. 37.____

38. If the fusible plug of a boiler is coated with scale, it will melt at a lower temperature. 38.____

39. A water pump is usually primed with oil or grease. 39.____

40. Sharp-edged hand tools should usually be carried with the sharp edge down. 40.____

41. Using chisels with mushroomed heads is a safe practice if the user wears safety goggles. 41.____

42. The fire in a boiler furnace should be cleaned before banking it for the night. 42.____

43. School classrooms usually require weekly scrubbing in order to keep them acceptably clean. 43.____

44. Trisodium phosphate is a poor cleaning agent for oily or greasy surfaces. 44.____

45. Weathering of coal is a source of fuel waste.   45.__

46. Standpipes usually supply water to the toilets and fountains on the upper floors of a   46.__
    building.

47. Goods subject to damage by heat should be stored near the ceiling of a storeroom if pos-   47.__
    sible.

48. Two light coats of wax on a floor are better than one good heavy coat.   48.__

49. If a custodian sees a child defacing a corridor wall, he should not stop the child but   49.__
    should report him to the principal or teacher.

50. A carbon tetrachloride fire extinguisher can be effectively used to put out a fire in an elec-   50.__
    tric motor.

KEY (CORRECT ANSWERS)

1.	T	11.	F	21.	F	31.	F	41.	F
2.	F	12.	T	22.	T	32.	F	42.	T
3.	F	13.	F	23.	T	33.	F	43.	F
4.	T	14.	F	24.	F	34.	F	44.	F
5.	F	15.	T	25.	T	35.	T	45.	T
6.	T	16.	F	26.	F	36.	T	46.	F
7.	F	17.	F	27.	F	37.	F	47.	F
8.	F	18.	F	28.	F	38.	F	48.	T
9.	T	19.	F	29.	T	39.	F	49.	F
10.	T	20.	T	30.	T	40.	T	50.	T

EXAMINATION SECTION
TEST 1

DIRECTIONS: Each question or incomplete statement is followed by several suggested answers or completions. Select the one that BEST answers the question or completes the statement. *PRINT THE LETTER OF THE CORRECT ANSWER IN THE SPACE AT THE RIGHT.*

1. The one of the following devices that is required on BOTH coal-fired and oil-fired boilers is a(n)

   1.____

   A. safety valve
   B. low water cut-off
   C. feed water regulator
   D. electrostatic precipitator

2. Lowering the thermostat setting by 5 degrees during the heating season will result in a fuel saving of MOST NEARLY _____ percent.

   2.____

   A. 2   B. 5   C. 20   D. 50

3. An electrically-driven rotary fuel oil pump must be protected from internal damage by the installation in the oil line of a

   3.____

   A. discharge-side strainer
   B. check valve
   C. suction gauge
   D. pressure relief valve

4. A float-thermostatic steam trap in a condensate return line that is operating properly will allow _____ to pass and will hold back _____.

   4.____

   A. steam and air; condensate
   B. air and condensate; steam
   C. steam and condensate; air
   D. steam; air and condensate

5. Changes in the combustion efficiency of a boiler can be determined by comparing changes in stack temperature and

   5.____

   A. steam pressure in the header
   B. over-the-fire draft
   C. percentage of carbon dioxide
   D. equivalent direct radiation

6. The classification of the coal that is USUALLY burned in school buildings is

   6.____

   A. anthracite
   B. bituminous
   C. semi-bituminous
   D. lignite

7. A boiler is equipped with the following pressurtrols:
   I.   Manual-reset pressurtrol
   II. Modulating pressurtrol
   III. High-limit pressurtrol
   The CORRECT sequence in which these devices should be actuated by rising steam pressure is:

   7.____

   A. I, II, III
   B. II, III, I
   C. III, I, II
   D. III, II, I

8. The temperature of the returning condensate in a low-pressure steam heating system is 195° F.
This temperature indicates that

    A. some radiator traps are defective
    B. some boiler tubes are leaking
    C. the boiler water level is too low
    D. there is a high vacuum in the return line

8.____

9. An over-the-fire draft gauge in a natural draft furnace is USUALLY read in

    A. feet per minute
    B. pounds per square inch
    C. inches of mercury
    D. inches of water

9.____

10. The equipment which is used to provide tempered fresh air to certain areas of a school building is a(n)

    A. exhaust fan
    B. window fan
    C. fixed louvre
    D. heating stack

10.____

11. A chemical FREQUENTLY used to melt ice on outdoor pavements is

    A. ammonia
    B. soda
    C. carbon tetrachloride
    D. calcium chloride

11.____

12. A herbicide is a chemical PRIMARILY used as a(n)

    A. disinfectant
    B. fertilizer
    C. insect killer
    D. weed killer

12.____

13. Established plants that continue to blossom year after year without reseeding are GENERALLY known as

    A. annuals
    B. parasites
    C. perennials
    D. symbiotics

13.____

14. A ferrous sulfate solution is sometimes used to treat shrubs or trees that have a deficiency of

    A. boron
    B. copper
    C. iron
    D. zinc

14.____

15. A tree is described as deciduous. This means PRIMARILY that it

    A. bears nuts instead of fruit
    B. has been pruned recently
    C. usually grows in swampy ground
    D. loses its leaves in the fall

15.____

16. If you are told that a container holds a 20-7-7 fertilizer, it is MOST likely that twenty percent of this fertilizer is

    A. nitrogen
    B. oxygen
    C. phosphoric acid
    D. potash

16.____

17. The landscape drawings for a school indicate the planting of <u>Acer platanoides</u> at a cer-   17._____
tain location on the grounds. Acer platanoides is a type of

    A. privet hedge   B. rose bush
    C. maple tree   D. tulip bed

18. A cleaner is attempting to lift a heavy drum of liquid cleaner from the floor to a shelf at   18._____
waist height.
He is MOST likely to avoid personal injury in lifting the drum if he

    A. keeps his back as straight as possible and lifts the weight primarily with his back
       muscles
    B. arches his back and lifts the weight primarily with his back muscles
    C. keeps his back as straight as possible and lifts the weight primarily with his leg
       muscles
    D. arches his back and lifts the weight primarily with his leg muscles

19. Of the following, the BEST first aid treatment for a cleaner who has burned his hand with   19._____
dry caustic lye crystals is to

    A. wash his hand with large quantities of warm water
    B. brush his hand lightly with a soft, clean brush and wrap it in a clean rag
    C. place his hand in a mild solution of ammonia and cool water
    D. wash his hand with large quantities of cold water

20. The purpose of the third prong in a three-prong electric plug used on a 120-volt electric   20._____
vacuum cleaner is to prevent

    A. serious overheating of the vacuum cleaner
    B. electric shock to the operator of the vacuum cleaner
    C. generation of dangerous microwaves by the vacuum cleaner
    D. sparking in the electric outlet caused by a loose electric plug

21. Of the following, the LEAST effective method for a school custodian to use to reduce win-   21._____
dow glass breakage in his school is to

    A. keep the area near the school free of sticks and stones
    B. consult with parents and civic organizations and request their assistance in reduc-
       ing breakage
    C. request that neighbors living near the school report after-hours incidents to the
       police department
    D. develop a reputation as a *tough guy* with the students so that they will be afraid to
       break windows in the school

22. The one of the following procedures that a school custodian should use when a tele-   22._____
phone caller makes a threat to place a bomb in the school building is to

    A. hang up on the caller
    B. keep the caller talking as long as possible and make notes on what he says
    C. tell the caller he has the wrong number
    D. tell the caller his voice is being recorded and the call is being traced to its source

23. A school custodian is responsible for enforcing certain safety regulations in the school.   23.____
The MOST important reason for enforcing safety regulations is that

    A. every accident can be prevented
    B. compliance with safety regulations will make all other safety efforts unnecessary
    C. safety regulations are the law, and law enforcement is an end in itself
    D. safety regulations are based on reason and experience with the best methods of accident prevention

24. The safety belts that are worn by cleaners when washing outside windows should be   24.____
inspected

    A. before each use   B. weekly
    C. monthly   D. semi-annually

25. The one of the following actions that a school custodian should take to help reduce bur-   25.____
glary losses in the school is to

    A. leave all the lights on in the school overnight
    B. see that interior and exterior doors are securely locked at the end of the day
    C. set booby traps that will severely injure anyone breaking in
    D. set up an apartment in the school basement and stay at the school every night

---

KEY (CORRECT ANSWERS)

1.	A		11.	D
2.	C		12.	D
3.	D		13.	C
4.	B		14.	C
5.	C		15.	D
6.	A		16.	A
7.	B		17.	C
8.	A		18.	C
9.	D		19.	D
10.	D		20.	B

21.	D
22.	B
23.	D
24.	A
25.	B

EXAMINATION SECTION
TEST 1

DIRECTIONS: Each question or incomplete statement is followed by several suggested answers or completions. Select the one that BEST answers the question or completes the statement. *PRINT THE LETTER OF THE CORRECT ANSWER IN THE SPACE AT THE RIGHT.*

1. In city schools, wiring for motors or lighting is

   A. 208-220 volt, 4 wire, 60 cycle
   B. 240-110 volt, 3 wire, 4 phase
   C. 120-208 volt, 3 phase, 4 wire
   D. 160-210 volt, 4 phase, 3 wire

   1._____

2. The LEAST likely cause of continuous vibration in a motor-driven pump is

   A. misalignment of motor and pump
   B. loose bearings in motor
   C. poor electric connection
   D. lack of graphite lubrication

   2._____

3. A starter for fluorescent lights should be ordered in

   A. volts   B. amps   C. current   D. watts

   3._____

4. A pipe is 50' long.
   If it drops 1/4" each foot, how many inches does it drop in 50'?

   A. 5.5   B. 8   C. 10   D. 12.5

   4._____

5. A plumber's friend operates by

   A. oscillation of water and air in the pipe
   B. density of water and pressure
   C. snake action
   D. water pressure *only*

   5._____

6. Compound is applied to pipe thread.
   When threading pipe, where would you apply compound?

   A. Male and female thread
   B. Female *only*
   C. Male *only*
   D. At the end of the male connection *only*

   6._____

7. A 6/32 thread refers to

   A. stove bolt   B. pipe thread
   C. machine thread   D. drill bit

   7._____

8. To hang a bulletin board on plaster or hollow tile wall, use

   A. self-tapping screws   B. wire cut nails
   C. expansion shields   D. molly shank and screw

   8._____

9. To relieve the vacuum on a pump, one of the following should operate: 9.____

    A. discharge valve   B. vacuum breaker
    C. foot valve   D. bleeder valve

10. When water in circulating line shows brown, the LIKELY cause is   10.____

    A. bacteria build-up
    B. rust
    C. sluggish circulation
    D. water treatment plant excessive chemical build-up

11. The purpose of rear chamber in an incinerator is for   11.____

    A. arresting sparks   B. removing noxious gases
    C. smoke reduction   D. an extra source of O_2

12. A stack switch will shut down an oil burner when   12.____

    A. the temperature of the oil is low
    B. steam pressure is too high
    C. there is flame failure
    D. oil pressure is low

13. A check valve in a low pressure boiler water line is to   13.____

    A. prevent contamination of boiler water
    B. prevent return flow of water
    C. equalize boiler water level
    D. prevent the pressure from increasing

14. A custodian should know   14.____

    A. how to repair equipment
    B. condition before breakdown
    C. right lubrication to use
    D. outside conditions

15. In removing grass stains from marble and wood, which of the following should be used?   15.____

    A. Oxalic acid   B. Muriatic acid
    C. Sodium silicate   D. Disodium silicate

16. If concrete cracks appear in spring and winter, the cause is MOST likely   16.____

    A. poor concrete mix
    B. too much foot traffic
    C. poor sub-soil drainage
    D. not enough room for expansion and contraction

17. Venetian blinds should be cleaned by   17.____

    A. using feather duster
    B. vacuuming
    C. washing with clear water
    D. washing with cleaning solution

18. To keep chrome-plated metal clean, you should 18._____

    A. polish with fine steel wool
    B. wash with soapy water and polish with soft cloth
    C. clean with scouring powder and polish with soft cloth
    D. none of the above

19. After wetting down the floor with water solution, the BEST mop to use is 19._____

    A. a mop wet with clean water
    B. one wrung out in solution water
    C. a dry mop
    D. one wrung out in clear water

20. After sweeping and dusting a room, the LAST thing that should be done is 20._____

    A. empty waste basket   B. switch off lights
    C. close windows   D. clean the furniture

21. A preheater is used to heat # _____ oil. 21._____

    A. 1   B. 2   C. 4   D. 6

22. If paint blisters on the wall, the MOST likely cause is 22._____

    A. too much paint   B. porous plaster
    C. moisture in wall   D. hair-line plaster cracks

23. Cracks in newly plastered walls should be filled with 23._____

    A. putty   B. rough plaster first
    C. spackling plaster   D. silicone gel-fill

24. The BEST reason for cleaning light bulbs is 24._____

    A. the bulb will last longer
    B. removing dust
    C. obtaining optimum light
    D. preventing electrical shock

25. The color of fire lines is 25._____

    A. yellow   B. green   C. brown   D. red

26. To neutralize acid soil, which of the following should be used? 26._____

    A. Nitrogen   B. Potash
    C. Phosphorus   D. Lime

27. A cleaning detergent is composed of 27._____

    A. cleaning acids   B. salts
    C. sodium compounds   D. alkaline compounds

28. The BEST method to use in watering trees and shrubs is to use   28.____

     A. jet-type velocity at roots
     B. hose with fine nozzle spray once a week and done well
     C. a hose only when needed to soak roots
     D. rotating single jet sprinkler

29. As a custodian, which of the following instructions would you give your staff in case of fire?   29.____

     A. Report to Principal
     B. Go to location and put out fire
     C. Pull nearest fire alarm station box
     D. Make sure each one knows in advance their assigned location of duty when alarm rings

30. Which of the following effects does a foam extinguisher have?   30.____

     A. Smothering   B. Cooling and smothering
     C. Wetting down   D. Insulating

31. The BEST fire extinguisher to use on electric motors is   31.____

     A. soda acid   B. foam type
     C. carbon dioxide   D. water

32. Two employees are arguing about their personal clothing locker. How would you handle this dispute?   32.____

     A. Reprimand both men
     B. Talk to them individually
     C. Speak to both of them together about it
     D. Write up a disciplinary report on both men

33. A fertilizer 5-10-5 means   33.____

     A. 5 potash - 10 nitrogen - 5 phosphorous
     B. 5 tobacco chip - 10 potash - 5 phosphoric acid
     C. 5 tobacco chip - 10 nitrogen - 5 potash
     D. 5 potassium - 10 nitrogen - 5 phosphorous

34. Sand gravel mix should be   34.____

     A. 1 sand, 2 gravel, 3 cement
     B. 1 cement, 2 gravel, 3 sand
     C. 1 cement, 2 sand, 3 gravel
     D. 2 cement, 3 sand, 2 gravel

35. _____ is found between the boiler and boiler safety valve.   35.____

     A. Check valve   B. No valve
     C. Steam stop valve   D. Regulating valve

KEY (CORRECT ANSWERS)

1.	B		16.	D
2.	C		17.	A
3.	D		18.	B
4.	D		19.	C
5.	A		20.	B
6.	C		21.	D
7.	C		22.	C
8.	C		23.	B
9.	B		24.	C
10.	C		25.	D
11.	C		26.	D
12.	C		27.	C
13.	A		28.	C
14.	B		29.	D
15.	A		30.	B

31.	C
32.	B
33.	A
34.	C
35.	B

TEST 2

DIRECTIONS: Each question or incomplete statement is followed by several suggested answers or completions. Select the one that BEST answers the question or completes the statement. *PRINT THE LETTER OF THE CORRECT ANSWER IN THE SPACE AT THE RIGHT.*

1.   Of the following, the BEST procedure in sweeping classroom floors is: 1._____

    A.   Open all windows before beginning the sweeping operation
    B.   The cleaner should move forward while sweeping
    C.   Alternate pull and push strokes should be used
    D.   Sweep under desks on both sides of an aisle while moving down the aisle

2.   Proper care of floor brushes includes   2._____

    A.   washing brushes daily after each use with warm soap solution
    B.   dipping brushes in kerosene periodically to remove dirt
    C.   washing with warm soap solution at least once a month
    D.   avoiding contact with soap or soda solutions to prevent drying of bristles

3.   An ADVANTAGE of vacuum cleaning rather than sweeping a floor with a floor brush is that   3._____

    A.   stationary furniture will not be touched by the cleaning tool
    B.   the problem of dust on furniture is reduced
    C.   the initial cost of the apparatus is less than the cost of an equivalent number of floor brushes
    D.   daily sweeping of rooms and corridors can be eliminated

4.   Sweeping compound for use on rubber tile, asphalt tile, or sealed wood floors must NOT contain   4._____

    A.   sawdust   B.   water
    C.   oil soap   D.   floor oil

5.   Of the following, the MOST desirable material to use in dusting furniture is a   5._____

    A.   soft cotton cloth   B.   hand towel
    C.   counter brush   D.   feather duster

6.   In high dusting of walls and ceiling, the CORRECT procedure is to   6._____

    A.   begin with the lower walls and proceed up to the ceiling
    B.   remove pictures and window shades only if they are dusty
    C.   clean the windows thoroughly before dusting any other part of the room
    D.   begin with the ceiling and then dust the walls

7.   When cleaning a classroom, the cleaner should   7._____

    A.   dust desks before sweeping
    B.   dust desks after sweeping
    C.   open windows wide during the desk dusting process
    D.   begin dusting at rows most distant from entrance door

8. Too much water on asphalt tile is objectionable MAINLY because the tile   8.____

    A. will tend to become discolored or spotted
    B. may be loosened from the floor
    C. tends to disintegrate prematurely
    D. becomes too slippery to walk on

9. To reduce the slip hazard resulting from waxing linoleum, the MOST practical of the following methods is to   9.____

    A. apply the wax in one heavy coat
    B. apply the wax after varnishing the linoleum
    C. buff the wax surface thoroughly
    D. apply the wax in several thin coats

10. Assume that the water-emulsion wax needed for routine waxing in your building is 15 gallons per month. This wax is supplied in 55 gallon drums.
To cover your needs for a year, the MINIMUM number of drums you should have to request is   10.____

    A. two   B. three   C. four   D. six

11. In washing down walls, the correct procedure is to start at the bottom of the wall and work to the top.
The MOST important reason for this is   11.____

    A. dirt streaking will tend to be avoided or easily removed
    B. less cleansing agent will be required
    C. rinse water will not be required
    D. the time for cleaning the wall is less than if washing started at the top of the wall

12. In mopping a wood floor of a classroom, the cleaner should   12.____

    A. mop against the grain of the wood wherever possible
    B. mop as large an area as possible at one time
    C. wet the floor before mopping with a cleaning agent
    D. mop only aisles and clear areas and use a scrub brush under desks and chairs

13. A precaution to observe in mopping asphalt file floors is: 13.____

    A. Keep all pails off such floors because they will leave water marks
    B. Do not wear rubber footwear while mopping these floors
    C. Use circular motion in rinsing and drying the floor to avoid streaking
    D. Never use a cleaning agent containing trisodium phosphate

14. The MOST commonly used cleansing agent for the removal of ink stains from a wood floor is   14.____

    A. kerosene   B. oxalic acid
    C. lye   D. bicarbonate of soda

15. The FIRST operation in routine cleaning of toilets and wash rooms is to 15.____

    A. wash floors
    B. clean walls
    C. clean wash basins
    D. empty waste receptacles

16. To eliminate the cause of odors in toilet rooms, the tile floors should be mopped with 16.____

    A. a mild solution of soap and trisodium phosphate in water
    B. dilute lye solution followed by a hot water rinse
    C. dilute muriatic acid dissolved in hot water
    D. carbon tetrachloride dissolved in hot water

17. The principal reason why soap should NOT be used in cleaning windows is that 17.____

    A. it causes loosening of the putty
    B. it may cause rotting of the wood frame
    C. a film is left on, the window, requiring additional rinsing
    D. frequent use of soap will cause the glass to become permanently clouded

18. The CHIEF value of having windows consisting of many small panes of glass is 18.____

    A. the window is much stronger
    B. accident hazards are eliminated
    C. cost of replacing broken panes is low
    D. cleaning windows consisting of small panes is easier than cleaning a window with a large undivided pane

19. Cleansing powders such as Ajax should not be used to clean and polish brass MAINLY because 19.____

    A. the brass turns a much darker color
    B. such cleansers have no effect on tarnish
    C. the surface of the brass may become scratched
    D. too much fine dust is raised in the polishing process

20. To remove chalk marks on sidewalks and cemented playground areas, the MOST acceptable cleaning method is 20.____

    A. using a brush with warm water
    B. using a brush with warm water containing some kerosene
    C. hosing down such areas with water
    D. using a brush with a solution of muriatic acid in water

21. The MOST important reason for oiling wood floors is that 21.____

    A. it keeps the dust from rising during the sweeping process
    B. the need for daily sweeping of classroom floors is eliminated
    C. oiled floors present a better appearance than waxed floors
    D. the wood surface will become waterproof and stain-proof

22. After oil has been sprayed on a wood floor, the sprayer should be cleaned before storing it.
The usual cleaning material for this purpose is

    A. ammonia water
    B. salt
    C. kerosene
    D. alcohol

22.____

23. The MOST desirable agent for routine cleaning of slate blackboards is

    A. warm water containing trisodium phosphate
    B. mild soap solution in warm water
    C. kerosene in warm water
    D. warm water alone

23.____

24. Neatsfoot oil is commonly used to

    A. oil light machinery
    B. prepare sweeping compound
    C. clean metal fixtures
    D. treat leather-covered chairs

24.____

25. Of the following daily jobs in the schedule of a custodian, the one he should do FIRST in the morning is to

    A. hang out the flag
    B. open all doors of the school
    C. fire boilers
    D. dust the principal's office

25.____

26. When a school custodian is newly assigned to a building at the start of the school term, his FIRST step should be to

    A. examine the building to determine needed maintenance and repair
    B. meet the principal and discuss plans for operation and maintenance of the building
    C. call a meeting of the teaching and custodial staff to explain his plans for the building
    D. review the records of maintenance and operation left by the previous custodian

26.____

27. A detergent is a material used GENERALLY for

    A. coating floors to resist water
    B. snow removal
    C. insulation of steam and hot water lines
    D. cleaning purposes

27.____

28. A good disinfectant is one that will

    A. have a clean odor which will cover up disagreeable odors
    B. destroy germs and create more sanitary conditions
    C. dissolve encrusted dirt and other sources of disagreeable odors
    D. dissolve grease and other materials that may cause stoppages in toilet waste lines

28.____

29. To help prevent leaks at the joints of water lines, the pipe threads are commonly covered with   29.____

    A. tar   B. cup grease
    C. rubber cement   D. white lead

30. The advantage of using screws instead of nails is that   30.____

    A. they have greater holding power
    B. they are available in a greater variety than are nails
    C. a hammer is not required for joining wood members
    D. they are less expensive

31. Of the following, the grade of steel wool that is the FINEST is   31.____

    A. 00   B. 0   C. 1   D. 2

32. The material used with solder to make it stick better is   32.____

    A. oakum   B. lye   C. oil   D. flux

33. In using a floor brush in a corridor, a cleaner should be instructed to   33.____

    A. use moderately long pull strokes whenever possible
    B. make certain that there is no overlap on sweeping strokes
    C. give the brush a slight jerk after each stroke to free it of loose dirt
    D. keep the sweeping surface of the brush firmly flat on the floor to obtain maximum coverage

34. A device installed in a drainage system to prevent gases from flowing into a building is called a   34.____

    A. trap   B. stall   C. cleanout   D. bidet

35. The plumbing fixture that contains a ball cock is the   35.____

    A. trap   B. water closet
    C. sprinkler   D. dishwasher

KEY (CORRECT ANSWERS)

1.	B		16.	A
2.	C		17.	C
3.	B		18.	C
4.	D		19.	C
5.	A		20.	A
6.	D		21.	A
7.	B		22.	C
8.	B		23.	D
9.	D		24.	D
10.	C		25.	C
11.	A		26.	B
12.	C		27.	D
13.	A		28.	B
14.	B		29.	D
15.	D		30.	A

31.	A
32.	D
33.	C
34.	A
35.	B

EXAMINATION SECTION
TEST 1

DIRECTIONS: Each question or incomplete statement is followed by several suggested
answers or completions. Select the one that BEST answers the question or
completes the statement. *PRINT THE LETTER OF THE CORRECT ANSWER
IN THE SPACE AT THE RIGHT.*

1. The safety device on an elevator door is called the   1._____

    A. governor   B. gate-switch
    C. interlock   D. safety fuse

2. Which of the following is the PROPER method of cleaning a room?   2._____

    A. Dust, empty wastebasket, sweep
    B. Empty wastebasket, dust, sweep
    C. Empty wastebasket, sweep, dust
    D. Sweep, dust, empty wastebasket

3. How would you determine when a waxed floor should be stripped?   3._____
When

    A. someone slipped on the floor
    B. wax builds up
    C. scuffs are not removed by buffing
    D. someone complains

4. To remove modelling plaster from the floor, you should use   4._____

    A. a sharp chisel
    B. a putty knife
    C. a floor scrubbing machine
    D. sulphuric acid

5. Which of the following floors would you NOT seal?   5._____

    A. Terrazzo   B. Cork   C. Asphalt   D. Tile

6. A mixing valve for domestic water blends   6._____

    A. cold water with hot boiler water
    B. hot and cold water
    C. cold water and hot water from coil submerged in boiler water
    D. hot and cold water from cooling coil

7. For sweeping under the radiators, the BEST tool to use is a   7._____

    A. dry mop   B. feather duster
    C. counter brush   D. floor broom

8. A wet return line is   8._____

    A. one containing air and water   B. above boiler water level
    C. below boiler water level   D. a condenser coil

9. A dry return line is   9.__

    A. one containing air *only*
    B. above boiler water level
    C. one containing air and water
    D. a line with a bleeder valve

10. The purpose of a fusetron is to   10.__

    A. provide motor starting current
    B. keep motor at rated speed
    C. protect from overload
    D. maintain constant motor speed

11. If combination faucet is in off position and water leaks from swivel, you should   11.__

    A. replace faucet washers
    B. repack swivel gland
    C. replace both washers and tighten swivel gland
    D. replace the faucet

12. The MAIN purpose of peat moss use is to   12.__

    A. improve soil condition
    B. fertilize soil
    C. help to keep soil moist
    D. retard the growth of weeds

13. Which of the following valves does NOT have a wheel and stem?   13.__

    A. Globe   B. Gate   C. Check   D. Plug cock

14. If a radiator is air-bound, the MOST likely cause is   14.__

    A. no condensate return
    B. defective steam valve
    C. defective air valve
    D. too much air carried in steam

15. The MAIN purpose of keeping accident reports on file is to   15.__

    A. have a record to show a lawyer
    B. contain cause of accident
    C. inform Principal of how it happened
    D. provide full information for official use

16. To repair a continually flushing flushometer, you should   16.__

    A. cut down on supply valve
    B. shut off water
    C. clean out flushometer
    D. replace defective parts

17. When a repair is required, the LEAST likely thing to be done is:　　17.____

    A. Determine if your staff can handle it
    B. Find out just what has to be done
    C. Ask for assistance from repair shops
    D. Decide which tools are needed to do the job

18. At which of the following locations should you find a remote control switch?　　18.____

    A. In principal's office
    B. In engineer's office
    C. At boiler room entrance
    D. At entrance to building

19. Sprinkler systems are more often found in the following location:　　19.____

    A. Boiler room
    B. Gym
    C. Storage rooms
    D. Science rooms

20. If a gas range flame is all whitish yellow, what does it indicate?　　20.____

    A. Insufficient gas pressure
    B. Insufficient air
    C. Not enough gas
    D. Too much air

21. If glass on water column breaks when boiler is operating, you should　　21.____

    A. bank fire
    B. shut off oil burner
    C. use tri-cocks
    D. close main steam valve

22. The BEST reason for setting a time limit on the job is　　22.____

    A. time available
    B. if completion is urgent
    C. if maximum output is effected this way
    D. the men are more likely to complete the job on time

23. The safety device on a gas line is called　　23.____

    A. gas cock
    B. automatic pilot
    C. solenoid valve
    D. safety shut-off valve

24. The MOST efficient boiler fuel operation is　　24.____

    A. low CO_2 high CO, low stack gas temperature
    B. high CO_2 low CO, low stack gas temperature
    C. high firebox temperature, high CO_2 high stack temperature
    D. high CO_2 low CO, high stack gas temperature

25. The central vacuum cleaning system should be cleaned　　25.____

    A. weekly
    B. twice weekly
    C. daily
    D. when necessary

26. If you had too much oil, what would you do for good combustion?　　26.____

    A. Increase secondary air
    B. Increase primary air
    C. Increase both
    D. Lower oil pressure

27. The purpose of blowing down the water column is to   27.____

    A. make sure there is enough water
    B. keep the gauge glass clean:
    C. determine the true water level
    D. make sure you have steam in boiler

28. Water hammer in water lines is caused by   28.____

    A. velocity of air and water
    B. defective faucet
    C. defective washers
    D. quick opening and closing of faucets

29. The CHIEF reason for a plumbing system trap is to   29.____

    A. equalize waste   B. provide good drainage
    C. provide water seal   D. none of the above

30. A vapor barrier is used for   30.____

    A. insulating electrically
    B. protecting against low temperature
    C. a moisture barrier
    D. exterior condensation on cold water pipes

31. The material recommended for removing blood or fruit stains from concrete is   31.____

    A. Soft soap   B. Neats foot oil
    C. Oxalic acid   D. Ammonia

32. For what purpose are panic bars used? To   32.____

    A. make sure door is locked
    B. provide easy exit
    C. meet Fire Department regulations
    D. keep door open

33. To detect a leak in the gas line, which of the following would you do?   33.____

    A. Call gas company   B. Use a soapy solution
    C. Use a lighted match   D. Smell the area

34. To preserve freshly laid concrete, you would   34.____

    A. cover it
    B. keep it moist
    C. keep it at a temperature of 60° F
    D. keep it at a temperature over 60° F

35. Gas is measured in   35.____

    A. thousands cubic feet
    B. hundreds cubic feet
    C. ten thousands cubic feet volume
    D. 100,000 cubic feet volume

36. The FIRST thing a window cleaner should do is   36.____

    A. test window bolts
    B. see that cleaning tools are good
    C. check window belt
    D. not lean too heavily on glass

37. Couplings on gas supply lines serve the same purpose as   37.____

    A. electrical conduit   B. machine threads
    C. right and left hand   D. water unions

38. Before a custodian leaves the building, he would be LEAST likely to   38.____

    A. lower the flag   B. remove hazards
    C. tidy the stock room   D. check all entry doors

39. Which of the following would you NOT use to paint chain-link fences?   39.____

    A. Brush   B. Sprayer
    C. Roller   D. None of the above

40. Which of the following steps should be taken in closing a low pressure boiler at the end   40.____
of heating season in preparation for lay-up?

    A. Empty water, close valves, drop fire
    B. Dump fire, close valves, let boiler cool, empty water
    C. Dump fire, let boiler cool, empty water, close valves
    D. None of the above

KEY (CORRECT ANSWERS)

1.	C	11.	A	21.	C	31.	D
2.	C	12.	C	22.	D	32.	B
3.	B	13.	C	23.	C	33.	B
4.	B	14.	C	24.	B	34.	B
5.	C	15.	D	25.	B	35.	A
6.	B	16.	D	26.	B	36.	C
7.	C	17.	C	27.	C	37.	C
8.	C	18.	C	28.	A	38.	C
9.	B	19.	C	29.	C	39.	B
10.	C	20.	D	30.	C	40.	B

TEST 2

DIRECTIONS: Each question or incomplete statement is followed by several suggested answers or completions. Select the one that BEST answers the question or completes the statement. *PRINT THE LETTER OF THE CORRECT ANSWER IN THE SPACE AT THE RIGHT.*

1. The lowest visible part of the water column attached to an HRT boiler should be AT LEAST   1.___

    A. 3 inches above the top row of tubes
    B. 6 inches above the fusible plug
    C. 1 inch above the top row of tubes
    D. 1/2 inch above the fusible plug

2. The function of a fusible plug is to   2.___

    A. melt if the water temperature is too high
    B. prevent too high a furnace temperature
    C. prevent excessive steam pressure from developing in the boiler
    D. melt when the water level drops below the level of the plug

3. To control the temperature of water in a domestic water supply tank, the device used is USUALLY a   3.___

    A. thermostat   B. pressuretrol
    C. solenoid valve   D. aquastat

4. A house trap is a device placed in the house drain immediately inside the foundation wall of the building. Its MAIN purpose is to   4.___

    A. trap sediment flowing in the house drain to the street sewer
    B. prevent sewer gases from circulating in the building plumbing system
    C. maintain air pressure balance in the vent lines of the plumbing system
    D. provide a means for cleaning the waste lines of the plumbing system

5. In the care and operation of steam boilers, a procedure that is considered GOOD practice is to   5.___

    A. open the safety valve in the event low water is found
    B. refill the boiler with cold water when the boiler is hot
    C. remove the boiler from service immediately if the water level cannot be determined because the gauge glass is broken
    D. use hot water where possible in refilling a boiler prior to firing

6. The addition of moisture to coal to promote combustion of coal is commonly referred to as   6.___

    A. tempering   B. dusting
    C. watering   D. dehumidifying

7. The purpose of fire doors in a building is to   7.___

    A. prevent fires   B. prevent arson
    C. avoid panic   D. prevent spread of fire

8. Of the following, the type of fire extinguisher that is MOST satisfactory for use on a fire in a place of operating electrical equipment is   8._____

    A. carbon dioxide   B. sand pail
    C. soda acid   D. foam

9. The device which is LEAST likely to be used by the custodian in cleaning minor stop-pages in the plumbing system is a   9._____

    A. snake   B. auger   C. plunger   D. trowel

10. The PROPER cleaning agent for a paint brush that has been used to shellac a floor is   10._____

    A. gasoline   B. linseed oil
    C. alcohol   D. turpentine

11. In cutting the ends of a number of lengths of wood at an angle of 45°, one would PREFERABLY use a   11._____

    A. protractor   B. triangle
    C. miter box   D. movable head T-square

12. To the custodian, the term *zeolite* refers to   12._____

    A. boiler insulation
    B. combustion chamber refactories
    C. boiler tube cleaning agent
    D. boiler water softening

13. A custodian notices a man in a corridor of the building. This visitor identifies himself as a police officer and states that he is observing a student in one of the classes.
The custodian should   13._____

    A. make no further inquiry of the police officer
    B. ask the police officer to check with the school principal if he has not already done so
    C. ask for all details, the name of the student, and reason for observation so that he can report the visit in his log book
    D. ask the police officer to leave the building unless he has received permission from the Board of Education in writing

14. When a paint coat blisters, the cause is USUALLY: 14._____

    A. Paint coat is too thick
    B. Plaster pores not sealed properly
    C. Moisture under the paint coat
    D. Too much oil in paint

15. Galvanized iron pails resist rusting because the surface of the iron is coated with   15._____

    A. copper   B. zinc   C. aluminum   D. lead

16. To maintain brick walls and to eliminate or prevent leaks, the walls are USUALLY   16._____

    A. painted   B. sprayed   C. pointed   D. refaced

17. A safety device that can be used instead of a fuse to protect a piece of electrical equip- 17.____
ment is a

    A. circuit breaker   B. rheostat
    C. toggle switch   D. relay

18. Custodians are required to abide by snow removal regulations, which state that snow be 18.____
removed

    A. from sidewalks within four hours after snow ceases to fall during daytime
    B. from sidewalks within 24 hours after snowfall ceases
    C. within a reasonable period only from walks immediately in front of school
       entrances
    D. from sidewalks within 12 hours only if the fall is greater than four inches

19. Which of the following types of grates should be used for ease in cleaning fires when 19.____
hand firing large boilers under natural draft at heavy loads with #1 buckwheat?

    A. Dumping grates
    B. Stationary grates with 3/4" air spaces
    C. Stationary grates (pinhole type)
    D. Shaking grates

20. Which of the following fuels contains the GREATEST number of heat units per pound? 20.____

    A. Hard coal   B. #6 fuel oil
    C. Yard screenings   D. Bituminous coal

21. The purpose of admitting air over the fire in a coal-fired furnace is USUALLY to 21.____

    A. reduce the stack gases temperature
    B. improve the draft
    C. reduce the smoke
    D. reduce the draft

22. In most usual types of large capacity oil burners using #6 oil, under fully automatic con- 22.____
trol, the atomization of the oil is produced by the

    A. pressure from the pump
    B. pressure from the secondary air fan
    C. oil temperature from the heater
    D. rotation of the burner assembly by the motor

23. Which of the following comes the closest to indicating the number of degree-days in a 23.____
normal heating season in New York City?

    A. 3000   B. 4000   C. 5000   D. 6000

24. A badly sooted HRT boiler under coal firing will show a _____ than a clean boiler. 24.____

    A. higher CO_2 value
    B. lower CO_2 value
    C. higher stack temperature
    D. lower draft loss

25. The direct room radiator in a school with a pneumatically controlled steam heating system is cold, while the adjoining rooms are heated adequately.
Of the following, the FIRST thing you would check in the room is the

    A. steam pipe in the room before the pneumatic steam valve
    B. thermostat
    C. pneumatic steam valve
    D. thermostatic trap

25._____

26. A vaporstat used on a fully automatic heavy oil burning rotary cup installation, with separate motor driven oil pump, is GENERALLY used to

    A. keep the boiler pressure within proper limits
    B. regulate the pressure of the primary air
    C. regulate the pressure of the secondary air
    D. shut down the burner when primary air failure occurs

26._____

27. Suppose that a small oil fire has broken out in the boiler room of your building.
Of the following, the one that is LEAST suitable as an extinguisher is

    A. soda acid
    B. pyrene (carbon tetrachloride)
    C. foamite
    D. carbon dioxide

27._____

28. An electric elevator car stalls on the ground floor of a school building.
Of the following, the item you would be LEAST likely to check in your inspection is

    A. *baby switch*
    B. floor door switch
    C. limit switch
    D. current to elevator motors

28._____

29. In an investigation of a complaint of sewer gas from a urinal in a regularly used toilet room, you find that the trap seal has been lost.
The LEAST common cause of this condition is

    A. evaporation of water from the trap
    B. vent blocked up
    C. high wind over roof vent
    D. self-siphonage

29._____

30. Of the following, the cleaning assignment which you would LEAST prefer to have performed during school hours is

    A. sweeping of corridors and stairs
    B. cleaning and polishing brass fixtures
    C. cleaning toilets
    D. dusting of offices, halls, and special rooms

30._____

31. BEST combustion conditions exist when the stack haze as indicated on the Ringelman chart scale is Number

    A. 1   B. 3   C. 5   D. 6

31._____

32. A pop safety valve is commonly a
    A. member with a rupture section
    B. dead weight valve
    C. ball and lever valve
    D. spring loaded valve

    32.____

33. Fusible plugs used as protective devices in HRT boilers producing low pressure steam should melt at temperatures
    A. above the temperature of the steam and below the temperature of the flue gases
    B. at the same temperature as the steam
    C. above the usual temperature of both the flue gases and the steam
    D. at about the same temperature as the flue gases

    33.____

34. The high low water alarm of a steam boiler is USUALLY located in the
    A. boiler   B. gauge glass
    C. water column   D. feedwater

    34.____

35. What is an advantage of shaking grates over stationary grates?
    A. The fire can be cleaned without opening the firedoor.
    B. They are warp-proof.
    C. They are usually more sturdily constructed than stationary grates.
    D. Deeper firebed can usually be maintained.

    35.____

36. An ACCEPTABLE method of detecting air leaks in the setting of a boiler is
    A. placing an open flame or burning torch near the point where the leaks are suspected
    B. coating the suspected parts of the setting with heavy grease
    C. coating the suspected points of leakage with a heavy soap emulsion
    D. inspecting suspected areas of leakage with a powerful light and hand magnifier

    36.____

37. In a plumbing installation, an escutcheon is a
    A. metal collar   B. reducing tee
    C. valve   D. single sweep

    37.____

38. A leaking faucet stem can be repaired by replacing the
    A. flange or the seat   B. nipple
    C. o-ring or the packing D. cock

    38.____

39. The abbreviation O.S. and Y, as used in plumbing, apply to a(n)
    A. hot well   B. radiator
    C. injector   D. gate valve

    39.____

40. Gas range piping should have a MINIMUM diameter of _____ inch.
    A. 3/4   B. 1/2   C. 1/4   D. 1/8

    40.____

KEY (CORRECT ANSWERS)

1.	A	11.	C	21.	C	31.	A
2.	D	12.	D	22.	D	32.	D
3.	D	13.	B	23.	C	33.	B
4.	B	14.	C	24.	C	34.	C
5.	C	15.	B	25.	A	35.	A
6.	A	16.	C	26.	D	36.	A
7.	D	17.	A	27.	A	37.	A
8.	A	18.	A	28.	C	38.	C
9.	D	19.	A	29.	A	39.	D
10.	C	20.	B	30.	D	40.	A

EXAMINATION SECTION
TEST 1

DIRECTIONS: Each question or incomplete statement is followed by several suggested answers or completions. Select the one that BEST answers the question or completes the statement. *PRINT THE LETTER OF THE CORRECT ANSWER IN THE SPACE AT THE RIGHT.*

1. In the wintertime, the FIRST thing a custodian does in the morning, after throwing the main switch, is to

    A. take a reading of the electric meter
    B. prepare his daily report of fuel consumption
    C. prepare sweeping compound
    D. inspect the water gauge of his boilers

1.____

2. Rubbish, stones, sticks, and papers on lawns in front of school buildings are MOST effectively collected by means of a

    A. 30 inch floor brush with thickly set bristles
    B. corn broom
    C. 4 foot pole with a nail set in the bottom of it
    D. rake

2.____

3. Which of the following statements about sweeping is NOT correct?

    A. Corridors and stairs should not be swept during school hours.
    B. Classrooms should usually be swept daily after the close of the afternoon session.
    C. Dry sweeping is not to be used in classrooms or corridors.
    D. Special rooms, as sewing rooms, may be swept during school hours if unoccupied.

3.____

4. The PROPER size of floor brush to be used in classrooms with fixed seats is _____ inches.

    A. 36   B. 24   C. 16   D. 6

4.____

5. Sweeping compound made of oiled sawdust should NOT be used on _____ floors.

    A. cement   B. rubber tile
    C. oiled wood   D. composition

5.____

6. In oiling a wood floor, it is GOOD practice to

    A. apply the oil with a dipped mop up to the baseboards of the walls
    B. avoid application of oil closer than 6 inches of the baseboards
    C. keep the oil about one inch from the baseboard
    D. make sure that oil is applied to the floors under radiators

6.____

7. Of the following, the LEAST desirable agent for cleaning blackboards is

    A. damp cloth
    B. clear warm water applied with a sponge
    C. warm water with a little kerosene
    D. warm water containing a mild soap solution

7.____

8. Chalk trays of blackboards should be washed and cleaned 8.____

    A. once a week
    B. daily
    C. only when the teacher reports cleaning needed
    D. once a month

9. In cleaning rooms by means of a central vacuum cleaning system, 9.____

    A. sweeping compound is used merely to prevent dust from rising
    B. rooms need cleaning only twice a week because the machine takes up the oil
    C. wood floors must be oiled more frequently as the machine takes up the oil
    D. the cleaner should not press down upon the tool but should guide it across the floor

10. A gas leak is suspected in the home economics class of a school. The procedure in locating the leak is to 10.____

    A. use a lighted match
    B. use a safety lamp
    C. place nose close to line and smell each section
    D. use soapsuds

11. The MOST important reason for placing asbestos jackets on steam lines is to 11.____

    A. prevent persons from burning their hands
    B. prevent heat loss
    C. protect the lines from injury
    D. make the lines appear more presentable

12. If the flag is used on a speaker's platform, it should be displayed 12.____

    A. above and behind the speaker
    B. as a drape over the front of the platform
    C. as a rosette over the speaker's head
    D. as a cover over the speaker's desk

13. When the flag of the United States of America is displayed from a staff projecting from the front of the building, it should be 13.____

    A. extended to the tip of the staff
    B. extended to about one foot from the tip of the staff
    C. secured so that there is a sag in the line
    D. extended slowly to the tip of the staff and then drawn back rapidly about 15 inches

14. The common soda-acid fire extinguisher should be checked and refilled 14.____

    A. every week   B. every month
    C. once a year   D. only if used

15. A small fire has broken out in an electric motor in a sump pump. The lubricant has apparently caught fire. The PROPER extinguisher to use is 15.____

    A. sand
    B. carbon tetrachloride (pyrene) fire extinguisher

C. soda-acid fire extinguisher
D. water under pressure from a hose

16. While cleaning windows, an employee falls from the fourth floor of the building to the sidewalk. The custodian finds the man unconscious.
The custodian should

   A. move the man into a more comfortable position near the wall of the building and then call a doctor
   B. try to revive the man by depressing his head slightly and applying artificial respiration
   C. hail a taxi and bring the man to a hospital for treatment
   D. phone for an ambulance and cover the man to keep him warm

16._____

17. The duties of a custodian include the knowledge of safety rules to prevent accidents and injuries to his employees and himself.
Of the following, the LEAST harmful practice is to

   A. carry a scraper in the pocket with the blade down
   B. measure the cleaning powder with your hands before placing the powder in water
   C. wet the hands before using steel wool
   D. use lye to clean paint brushes

17._____

18. The MOST important reason for not wringing out a mop by hand is that

   A. water cannot be removed effectively in this way
   B. it is not fair to the cleaner
   C. the dirt remains on the mop after the water is removed
   D. pins, nails, or other sharp objects may be picked up and cut the hand, causing an infection

18._____

19. The method of using a ladder which you would consider LEAST safe is:

   A. Grasping the side rails of the ladder instead of the rungs when going up
   B. To see that the door is secured wide open when working on a ladder at a door
   C. Leaning weight toward ladder while working on it
   D. Standing on top of the ladder to reach working place

19._____

20. When a window pane is broken, the FIRST step the custodian takes is to

   A. remove broken glass from floors and window sill
   B. determine the cause
   C. remove the putty with a putty knife
   D. prepare a piece of glass to replace the broken pane

20._____

21. Your instructions to a cleaner about the proper sweeping of offices should include the following instruction:

   A. Do not move chairs and wastebaskets from their places when sweeping
   B. Place chairs and baskets on the desks to get them out of the way
   C. Set aside the loose small furniture and chairs in an orderly manner when sweeping office floors
   D. Move the desks and chairs to the side of the room close to the wall in order to sweep properly

21._____

22. To remove dirt accumulations after the completion of the sweeping task, brushes should be   22.____

     A. tapped on the floor in the normal sweeping position
     B. struck on the floor against the side of the block
     C. struck on the floor against the end of the block
     D. turned upside down and the handle tapped on the floor

23. To sweep rough cement floors in a basement, the BEST tool to use is a   23.____

     A. deck brush   B. new 30" floor brush
     C. corn broom   D. treated mop

24. When a floor is scrubbed, it is NOT correct to   24.____

     A. use a steady, even rotary motion
     B. rinse the floor with clean hot water
     C. have the mop strokes follow the boards when drying the floor
     D. wet the floor first by pouring several bucketsful of water on it

25. Flushing with a hose is MOST appropriate as a method of cleaning   25.____

     A. terrazzo floors of corridors
     B. untreated wood floors
     C. linoleum floors where not in frequent use
     D. cement floors

KEY (CORRECT ANSWERS)

1.	D		11.	B
2.	D		12.	A
3.	A		13.	A
4.	C		14.	C
5.	B		15.	B
6.	D		16.	D
7.	C		17.	A
8.	A		18.	D
9.	D		19.	D
10.	D		20.	A

21.	C
22.	A
23.	C
24.	D
25.	D

TEST 2

DIRECTIONS: Each question or incomplete statement is followed by several suggested answers or completions. Select the one that BEST answers the question or completes the statement. *PRINT THE LETTER OF THE CORRECT ANSWER IN THE SPACE AT THE RIGHT.*

Questions 1-5.

DIRECTIONS: Column I lists cleaning jobs. Column II lists cleansing agents and devices. Select the proper cleansing agent from Column II for each job in Column I. Place the letter of the cleansing agent selected in the space at the right corresponding to the number of the cleansing job.

COLUMN I

COLUMN II

1. Chewing gum
   A. Muriatic acid
   B. Broad bladed knife
2. Ink stains
   C. Kerosene
   D. Oxalic acid
3. Fingermarks on glass
   E. Lye
   F. Linseed oil
4. Rust stains on porcelain

5. Hardened dirt on porcelain

1.____

2.____

3.____

4.____

5.____

6. When the bristles of a floor brush have worn short, the brush should be   6.____

   A. thrown away and the handles saved
   B. saved and the brush used on rough cement floors
   C. saved and used for high dusting in classrooms
   D. saved and used for the weekly scrubbing of linoleum floors

7. Feather dusters should NOT be used because they   7.____

   A. take more time to use than other dusters
   B. cannot be cleaned
   C. do not take up the dust but merely move it from one place to another
   D. do not stir up the dust and streak the furniture with dust rails

8. Floors that are usually NOT waxed are those made of   8.____

   A. pine wood
   B. mastic tile
   C. rubber tile
   D. terrazzo

9. For sweeping under radiators and other inaccessible places, the MOST appropriate tool is the   9.____

   A. counter brush
   B. dry mop
   C. feather duster
   D. 16" floor brush

10. A cleansing agent that should NOT be used in the cleaning of windows is   10.____

    A. water containing fine pumice
    B. water containing a small amount of ammonia
    C. water containing a little kerosene
    D. a paste cleanser made from water and cleaning powder

11. The BEST way to dust desks is to use a   11.____

    A. circular motion with soft dry cloth that has been washed
    B. damp cloth, taking care not to disturb papers on the desk
    C. soft cloth, moistened with oil, using a back and forth motion
    D. back and forth motion with a soft dry cloth

12. Trisodium phosphate is a substance BEST used in   12.____

    A. washing kalsomined walls
    B. polishing of brass
    C. washing mastic tile floors
    D. clearing stoppages

13. Treated linoleum is PROPERLY cleaned by daily   13.____

    A. dusting with a treated mop
    B. sweeping with a floor brush
    C. mopping with a weak soap solution
    D. mopping after removal of dust with a floor brush

14. Of the following, the MOST proper use for chamois skin is   14.____

    A. drying of window glass after washing
    B. washing of window glass
    C. polishing of metal fixtures
    D. drying toilet bowls after washing

15. A squeegee is a tool which is used in   15.____

    A. clearing stoppages in waste lines
    B. the central vacuum cleaning system
    C. cleaning inside boiler surfaces
    D. drying windows after washing

16. Concrete and cement floors are usually painted a battleship gray color.   16.____
The MOST important reason for painting the floor is

    A. to improve the appearance of the floor
    B. the paint prevents the absorption of too much water when the floor is mopped
    C. the paint makes the floor safer and less slippery
    D. the concrete becomes harder and will not settle

17. After a sweeping assignment is completed, floor brushes should be stored   17.____

    A. in the normal sweeping position, bristles resting on the floor
    B. by hanging the brushes on pegs or nails

C. by piling the brushes on each other carefully in a horizontal position
D. in a dry place after a daily washing

18. Painted walls and ceilings should be brushed down   18._____

    A. daily
    B. weekly
    C. every month, especially during the winter
    D. two or three times a year

19. If an asphalt tile floor becomes excessively dirty, the method of cleaning should include   19._____

    A. the use of kerosene or benzine as a solvent
    B. the use of a solution of modified laundry soda
    C. sanding down the spotted areas with a sanding machine on the wet floor
    D. use of a light oil and treated mop

20. To remove light stains from marble walls, the BEST method is to   20._____

    A. use steel wool and a scouring powder, then rinse with clear warm water
    B. wash the stained area with a dilute acid solution
    C. sand down the spot first, then wash with mild soap solution
    D. wet marble first, then scrub with mild soap solution using a soft fiber brush

21. To rid a toilet room of objectionable odors, the PROPER method is to   21._____

    A. spread some chloride of lime on the floor
    B. place deodorizer cubes in a box hung on the wall
    C. wash the floor with hot water containing a little kerosene
    D. wash the floor with hot water into which some disinfectant has been poured

22. Toilet rooms, to be cleaned properly, should be swept   22._____

    A. daily
    B. and mopped daily
    C. daily and mopped twice a week
    D. daily and mopped thoroughly at the end of the week

23. In waxing a floor, it is usually BEST to   23._____

    A. start the waxing under stationary furniture and then do the aisles
    B. pour the wax on the floor, spreading it under the desks with a wax mop
    C. remove the old wax coat before rewaxing
    D. wet mop the floor after the second coat has dried to obtain a high polish

24. The BEST reason why water should not be used to clean kalsomined walls of a boiler   24._____
room is that the

    A. walls are usually not smooth and will hold too much water
    B. kalsomine coating does not hold dust
    C. kalsomine coating will dissolve in water and leave streaks
    D. wall brick and kalsomine coating will not dissolve in water and so cannot be
       cleaned

25. In mopping a floor, it is BEST practice to   25.____

    A. swing the mop from side to side, using the widest possible stroke across the floor up to the baseboard
    B. swing the mop from side to side, using the widest possible stroke across the floor surface, stopping the stroke from 3 to 5 inches from baseboards
    C. use short, straight strokes, up and back, stopping the strokes about 5 inches from the baseboards
    D. use short straight strokes, up and back, stopping the strokes at the baseboard

—————

KEY (CORRECT ANSWERS)

1.	B		11.	D
2.	D		12.	C
3.	C		13.	A
4.	A		14.	A
5.	C		15.	D
6.	B		16.	B
7.	C		17.	B
8.	D		18.	D
9.	A		19.	D
10.	A		20.	D

21.	D
22.	B
23.	A
24.	C
25.	B

—————

EXAMINATION SECTION
TEST 1

DIRECTIONS: Each question or incomplete statement is followed by several suggested answers or completions. Select the one that BEST answers the question or completes the statement. *PRINT THE LETTER OF THE CORRECT ANSWER IN THE SPACE AT THE RIGHT.*

1. Roaches are LEAST likely to be found in

    A. toilet rooms   B. locker rooms
    C. offices   D. waste paper rooms

1.____

2. A star drill is used to

    A. cut an old nipple from a fitting
    B. groove metal
    C. drill holes in stone and brick
    D. drill star-shaped holes in hard wood

2.____

3. A flushometer is a device which

    A. measures the velocity of flow of water through a toilet fixture
    B. acts as a valve in low tanks on water closet
    C. acts as a valve in high tanks on water closet
    D. releases water to flush water closets of the tankless type

3.____

4. The type of valve which LEAST obstructs the flow of water in water lines is the _____ valve.

    A. gate   B. pressure regulating
    C. angle   D. globe

4.____

5. The purpose of a sump pump is to

    A. lift cellar drainage into a sewer
    B. clear a stoppage in a toilet fixture
    C. empty radiators of water condensate
    D. keep water pressure in boilers constant

5.____

6. A bibb reseater is used in the repair of

    A. faucets   B. gate valves
    C. scaly fusible plugs   D. check valves

6.____

7. A *plumber's friend* is a device used to clear a stoppage in a

    A. drainage line   B. vent line
    C. house sewer   D. water supply fixture

7.____

8. Which of the following statements about tools and their uses is INCORRECT?

    A. A wrench should never be used as a hammer.
    B. A screwdriver should not be used as a chisel.
    C. When removing a bit from a hole after boring, turn the bit all the way.
    D. Before using a chisel, make sure that the head is mushroomed.

8.____

Questions 9-12.

DIRECTIONS: Column I lists tools used by a custodian. The uses of tools are given in Column II. Select the CORRECT use for the tools listed and place the letter representing your choice next to the number of the tool in the space at the right.

<u>COLUMN I</u>

9.   Center punch

10. Cold chisel

11. Rip saw

12. Allen wrench

<u>COLUMN II</u>

A.   Punch round holes in center of metal sheets

B.   Turn headless set screws

C.   Mark location of a hole to be drilled

D.   Cut wood parallel or with the grain

E.   Cut across the grain of wood

F.   Cut off a rivet head

G.   Turn flat-head wood screws

9. _C_

10. _F_

11. _D_

12. _B_

13. To hold a piece of lumber in place, the length of nail should be _____ the thickness of the lumber.

     A.   three times
     C.   one and one-half times
     B.   equal to
     D.   half

13. _A_

14.

14. _D_

METER READING AT BEGINNING OF PERIOD

METER READING AT END OF PERIOD

The above are the readings on the electric meter at the beginning and end of a period. The TOTAL kilowatt hour consumption is

A.   264   B.   570   C.   61   D.   175

15. Proper combustion of fuel is obtained when   15.____

    A. the flue gases contain a large percentage of carbon monoxide
    B. black smoke appears in the flue gases
    C. there is 10 to 15 percent carbon dioxide in the flue gases
    D. the flame of the fire is high enough to reach the fire tubes

16. The vertical pipes leading from the steam mains to the radiators are called   16.____

    A. expansion joints   B. radiant coils
    C. drip lines   D. risers

17. Try cocks are used to   17.____

    A. determine the exact water level in the boiler
    B. find the approximate water level in the boiler
    C. learn if steam is being generated in the boiler
    D. obtain an approximate idea of the steam pressure

18. If a ton of anthracite coal occupies approximately 40 cubic feet, the space required, in cubic yards, for 135 tons of coal is   18.____

    A. 200   B. 128.6   C. 600   D. 40

19. During the winter heating season, it is BEST practice to blow down the boiler   19.____

    A. once a month
    B. twice daily
    C. only when new grates are installed
    D. once a day

20. A boiler blow-off valve is PRIMARILY used to   20.____

    A. maintain constant boiler pressure
    B. drain water from boiler
    C. allow air to enter boiler when proper temperature is reached
    D. reduce boiler pressure

21. When a room becomes heated above the upper temperature setting of a thermostat which controls a check damper, the damper is   21.____

    A. automatically closed to reduce the air supply
    B. opened to admit more air
    C. not affected, but the supply of the boiler is increased
    D. partially closed and the water supply of the boiler is increased

22. When a custodian finds that the water level of his boiler is dangerously low, he should   22.____

    A. open his drafts
    B. immediately fill boiler with cold water
    C. cover the fire with wet ashes
    D. close all air openings to the fire box

23. Which one of the following is NOT a good method in banking fires?   23.____

    A. A little ash should be left on that portion of the fire not banked.
    B. The coal should be covered with ashes to preserve the fire.
    C. The dampers should be closed except for a small opening to admit a little air.
    D. Ashes should be removed from the ashpit.

24. Radiators radiate more heat when they are painted with   24.____

    A. bronze paint   B. aluminum paint
    C. regular wall paint   D. shellac

25. When a boiler is laid up for the summer, one of the things NOT to do is   25.____

    A. tap brace and stary rods with a hammer to detect loose rods
    B. leave water in boiler if basement is damp
    C. close all hand holes and manholes to prevent dust and air from getting into the cleaned boiler
    D. clean gauge glasses with muriatic acid to dissolve the accumulations of lime and other deposits

---

KEY (CORRECT ANSWERS)

1. C		11. D
2. C		12. B
3. D		13. A
4. A		14. D
5. A		15. C
6. A		16. D
7. A		17. B
8. D		18. A
9. C		19. D
10. F		20. B

21. B
22. C
23. B
24. B
25. C

TEST 2

DIRECTIONS: Each question or incomplete statement is followed by several suggested answers or completions. Select the one that BEST answers the question or completes the statement. *PRINT THE LETTER OF THE CORRECT ANSWER IN THE SPACE AT THE RIGHT.*

1. A heating plant is to be laid up for the summer.
   With respect to fire surfaces, the PROPER procedure after cleaning is to   1._____

   A. keep them moist with water applied with a spray
   B. paint them with a good plastic paint
   C. coat them with oil
   D. paint them with a metallic paint

2. When starting a fire in the boiler, the custodian should   2._____

   A. have ashpit doors and dampers closed before firing to give proper draft
   B. place about one inch of coal directly on the grate and then ignite with oil waste placed on top of the coal
   C. keep dampers closed and ashpit doors open to obtain proper drafts
   D. spread a bed of coal about three inches thick on the grates and then build fire on this bed

3. The vacuum system of storm heating does NOT have   3._____

   A. air valves on radiators
   B. thermostatic traps on radiators
   C. drip traps
   D. steam risers connected to radiators

4. The capacity of a heating boiler is USUALLY expressed in terms of   4._____

   A. square feet of radiation
   B. cubic feet of steam
   C. pounds of steam per hour
   D. the number of radiators required

5. The hammering noise in a heating system is caused by   5._____

   A. the pressure of water acting against the walls of the water pipe supplying the boiler
   B. contact of steam and water in the radiators
   C. the vibration of loose fire tubes in the boiler
   D. the vacuum effect of the release of water in the steam gauge

6. In one hour, one square foot of grate for a tubular boiler will burn, with natural draft, about _____ lbs. of hard coal.   6._____

   A. 12   B. 25   C. 6   D. 30

7. When priming occurs in a boiler,   7._____

   A. the fire will be extinguished
   B. the steam becomes superheated and too dry
   C. the fire tubes become overheated and may crack
   D. water particles are carried over with the steam into the steam lines

8. One of the ways to prevent or reduce the amount of smoke from a furnace is to 8.___

    A. reduce the quantity of air supplied to the fire box
    B. supply coal in large quantities and no more than twice a day
    C. cool the fire bed to prevent high temperatures in the fire box
    D. keep live coals at the top of the fire bed

9. Of the following, the SMALLEST size coal is 9.___

    A. chestnut   B. egg   C. buckwheat   D. pea

10. If coal is to be stored, the following precaution should be followed: 10.___

    A. Coal should be piled in conical piles rather than horizontal layers
    B. Coal should be placed in storage on hot summer days
    C. Avoid alternate wetting and drying of coal
    D. Coal should be piled no more than three feet deep

11. The HRT boiler contains 11.___

    A. fire tubes in which hot gases flow
    B. water tubes in which water flows to form steam
    C. no horizontal return tubes
    D. no way in which a vacuum return can be connected

12. A classroom is properly heated in the winter time when the temperature is about _____ 12.___
$^{\circ}$F and the relative humidity is _____%.

    A. 70; 40 to 60   B. 78; 40 to 60   C. 65; 30   D. 75; 90

13. The average temperature on a day in January is 30° F. 13.___
This would be called a _____ degree day.

    A. 40   B. 35   C. 30   D. 25

14. The term BTU is used in connection with 14.___

    A. heating quality of a fuel   B. the size of boiler tubes
    C. radiator fittings   D. heating qualities of radiators

15. Which one of the following is NOT the cause of clinker formation? 15.___

    A. Poor quality coal
    B. Thick fires
    C. Closed ashpit doors
    D. Water sprayed into the ashpit at intervals during the day

16. When a spot has burned through the fire bed, it is a GOOD plan to 16.___

    A. fill the burned out hole with green coal
    B. push burning coals to that part of the grate before spreading green coal on it
    C. fill that part of the grate with cold ashes, then place green coal on it
    D. fill the spot with excelsior and then place green coal on it

17. Thin spots or holes in a fire bed are USUALLY

  17.____

  A. developed in the front part or center of the fire bed
  B. developed near the back or corners of the fire bed
  C. located where there is a smoky, dull flame
  D. the result of burning soft coal

18. With respect to the operation of univents, the custodian should

  18.____

  A. close the steam valve supplying the unit radiators at the close of school every day
  B. see that the steam valve supplying the unit radiators is never closed except when repairs are required
  C. shut off the univents at the close of the day by pulling the main switch
  D. make certain that no part of the univent has water in it

19. Ventilating systems for toilets usually should be separate from the building ventilating system because

  19.____

  A. it prevents toilet odors from reaching rooms
  B. toilets need a more dependable ventilating system
  C. the requirements of the two systems are different
  D. only the toilets need ventilating in summer

20. When the flues of a boiler require frequent cleaning, the PROBABLE cause is

  20.____

  A. excess draft
  B. too high a rate of combustion
  C. incomplete combustion
  D. lack of clinker formation

21. Generally, the part of the building where the highest temperature is maintained in the wintertime is the

  21.____

  A. corridors   B. toilets
  C. gymnasium   D. regular classrooms

22. A template is a

  22.____

  A. round disc used to close openings in walls where a fixture has been removed
  B. pattern that has been cut, bent, or molded to a definite shape and size
  C. plate used under machines or motors to catch excess oil
  D. metal form to be placed behind radiators to protect the wall

23. A student slips on the floor of the entrance to the school building. A lawyer representing the family of the child asks for information concerning the accident. The custodian should

  23.____

  A. be cooperative and give all details concerning the accident and the condition of the entrance
  B. tell the lawyer that he will give the desired information if the child's parents give their consent
  C. refer the lawyer to the legal division of the Board of Education for information concerning the matter
  D. refuse to allow the lawyer to enter the school building

24. A teacher tells you that waxing a rubber tile floor is dangerous because the floor becomes too slippery. Your response should be 24.___

    A. that the children should be careful in walking on these floors and should wear rubber heels to avoid slipping
    B. an explanation of the non-slipping properties of a water emulsion wax properly applied
    C. tell her to mind her own business
    D. that it is not dangerous because no children have fallen and injured themselves

25. To order wet mop filler replacements, a custodian should specify the 25.___

    A. number of strands   B. girth
    C. weight   D. wet test strength

———————

KEY (CORRECT ANSWERS)

1.	C		11.	A
2.	D		12.	A
3.	A		13.	B
4.	A		14.	A
5.	B		15.	D
6.				
7.				
8.				
9.				
10.				

———————

EXAMINATION SECTION
TEST 1

DIRECTIONS: Each question or incomplete statement is followed by several suggested answers or completions. Select the one that BEST answers the question or completes the statement. *PRINT THE LETTER OF THE CORRECT ANSWER IN THE SPACE AT THE RIGHT.*

1. Which of the following chemicals is used to decrease the amount of oxygen in boiler water?   1.____

   A. Soda ash   B. Sodium chloride
   C. Sodium sulfite   D. Trisodium phosphate

2. The house tank in the basement of your school building has a pressure gauge 10 feet above the bottom of the tank. If a column of water weighs .434 pounds per square inch per foot and the pressure gauge reads 47 pounds per square inch, then the pressure on the booster pump at the base of the tank is MOST NEARLY, in pounds per square inch,   2.____

   A. 47   B. 52   C. 57.50   D. 61.25

3. Assume that a shipment of ammonia and bleach have just been delivered to your school and one of your cleaners asks to be instructed as to how the ammonia and bleach are to be stored.   3.____
   You should instruct him to store them

   A. *together,* because liquids are usually stored with other liquids
   B. *separately,* because shelf life is increased when supplies are maintained in their own areas away from other supplies
   C. *together,* because it is easier to keep an accurate inventory when supplies that are delivered together are stored together
   D. *separately,* because their containers could break and mix, creating a highly toxic gas

4. Of the following, which one is the MOST effective technique for motivating your employees?   4.____

   A. Regularly remind them that they receive a good salary and other benefits
   B. Publicly commend employees when they do good work
   C. Socialize with them during breaks and after working hours
   D. Overlook minor infractions and ignore rules that you disagree with

5. Which of the following chemicals is used to melt ice and snow?   5.____

   A. Calcium chloride   B. Soda ash
   C. Trisodium soot   D. Sodium sulphite

6. Boiler *handholes* are used for   6.____

   A. climbing onto boilers   B. lighting burners
   C. cleaning soot   D. inspecting boilers

7. The true water level for a boiler in operation is determined by operating the   7.____

   A. pressure relief valve   B. blow down valve
   C. aquastat   D. tri-cocks

8. There have been a number of illegal entries into your building during school hours, and the school principal asks you to padlock certain exit doors in the building to control such entry. You and the principal are both aware that there are laws prohibiting the padlocking of exit doors, but the principal maintains that closing off the doors in question would not impede easy exit from your building.
You should

   A. have the doors locked as requested but also inform your supervisor as to your decision to do so and your reason for that decision
   B. refuse to have the doors locked and if the principal insists, refer him to your supervisor
   C. have the doors locked if, after looking into the matter, you determine that the remaining unlocked doors would be sufficient
   D. refuse to have the doors locked unless the principal overrules you and puts it in writing

8.____

9. You are in the boiler room when a steam line ruptures and the water in the gauge glass disappears.
Of the following, your FIRST action should be to

   A. secure the fire
   B. shut down the vacuum pump
   C. add water to replace the escaping water
   D. secure the steam valve

9.____

10.

The reading of the above gas meter diagram is

   A. 6929   B. 6939   C. 7929   D. 7939

10.____

11. Sight glasses are found

   A. on air compressors
   B. in classroom doors
   C. in cross-corridor doors
   D. on vision panels

11.____

12. Graphite is USUALLY used as a

   A. lubricant   B. cleaning compound
   C. sealant   D. boiler water additive

12.____

13. If you receive a yearly allowance of $52,000 for your school, what would MOST NEARLY be your bi-weekly allowance if you determined that figure based on a year of 365 days?

   A. $1,925.28   B. $1,961.30   C. $1,994.52   D. $2,000.00

13.____

14. Number 6 fuel oil is also known as

14.____

    A. crude oil   B. bunker C oil
    C. gas oil   D. kerosene

15. Of the following CO_2 readings, which one indicates the LOWEST excess in the flue gas?

15.____

    A. 10.0%   B. 12.0%   C. 14.0%   D. 15.0%

16. A large section of a ceiling in an occupied classroom is hanging loosely.
Of the following, which is the FIRST action you should take?

16.____

    A. Check for leaks in the floor above
    B. Have the ceiling replastered immediately
    C. Prepare a requisition for repair
    D. Have the room evacuated

17. If you sometimes enforce rules with strong disciplinary action and at other times you enforce the same rules with mild disciplinary action, your practice is a

17.____

    A. *good* one, because it enables you to apply strict discipline to cleaners who accept it and to avoid confrontations with your more resistant workers
    B. *bad* one, because generally speaking strong disciplinary actions should be taken for infractions
    C. *good* one, because employees who are *kept guessing* about what supervisors are thinking are less likely to try to take advantage
    D. *bad* one, because discipline should be applied with consistency

18. If one of your employee's gross salary is $38,000 a year and you must deduct 5.85% of that sum, you should deduct

18.____

    A. $2223.00   B. $2226.00   C. $2235.00   D. $2342.00

19. The remote control switch of an oil burning heating plant should be located

19.____

    A. at the boiler room exit door
    B. in the custodian's office
    C. between 2 and 5 feet from the boiler
    D. on the boiler at eye level

20. Fire Department personnel, while making a routine inspection, issue violations for conditions existing in your building.
Of the following, it is MOST appropriate for you to

20.____

    A. explain that because schools are city property, violations cannot be issued
    B. accept the violations as written and take follow-up action
    C. inform them that they must go through proper channels before issuing the violations
    D. volunteer information about other conditions possibly in violation

21. Assume that your school building has three-phase wiring. Assume also that when you throw the start-up switch on a motor in your boiler room, the motor hums but does not turn.
Of the following, the MOST likely cause for this is

    A. low voltage
    B. motor grounding
    C. low amperage
    D. a blown fuse

21.____

22. Two of your cleaners are entitled to retroactive pay of 18 cents per hour. One of the cleaners is to be paid retroactive money for 800 hours at straight time and 50 hours at time and a half. The other cleaner is entitled to 750 hours at straight time and 100 hours at time and a half.
What is the TOTAL amount of retroactive money to be paid to the two employees?

    A. $238.50   B. $265.90   C. $319.50   D. $346.50

22.____

23. Of the following, the MOST likely cause of coal gas fumes is a(n)

    A. improperly banked fire
    B. high steam pressure
    C. improper water level
    D. heavy BTU content in coal being used

23.____

24. Boiler draft is measured in

    A. pounds per square inch
    B. degrees Fahrenheit
    C. inches of water
    D. cubic feet per minute

24.____

25. Of the following, which method should be used to check a CO_2 fire extinguisher?

    A. Discharge it
    B. Weigh it
    C. Read the gauge
    D. Shake it

25.____

26. A(n) _____ pump is used on a boiler system using number 6 oil.

    A. transfer   B. vacuum   C. ejector   D. sump

26.____

27. Your boiler water has a pH of 8. This means that the water is

    A. acidic   B. neutral   C. alkaline   D. dirty

27.____

28. Assume that the high temperature on March 14 was 72° F and the low temperature was 52° F. The standard temperature for calculation of degree days is 65° F.
The number of degree days for March 14 is

    A. 3   B. 7   C. 13   D. 20

28.____

29. Pig tails are commonly found on

    A. steam gauges
    B. water meters
    C. temperature recorders
    D. draft gauges

29.____

30. Your school principal complains to you that a workman making repairs to the windows in your building is making noise that is disrupting classroom instruction.
Of the following, the FIRST action you should take is to

    A. ignore the principal in the hope that the noise subsides
    B. tell the principal that there has to be a certain amount of noise when repair work is being done
    C. meet with the workman to discuss rescheduling the work in order to minimize disruption
    D. inform the workman's supervisor that you have received complaints and warn him that you will take further action if he fails to cooperate

30.____

31. *Checkerboard* floors are found in

    A. restrooms
    B. boiler rooms
    C. classrooms
    D. lunchrooms

31.____

32. One of your cleaners has a gross bi-weekly salary of $736.94.
If the federal tax deduction for that period is $127.92, the state tax deduction is $42.85, and the FICA is $61.02, the city decusion is $7.36 and the state disability is $.60, what is the cleaner's net pay?

    A. $239.75   B. $362.49   C. $497.19   D. $521.03

32.____

33. The operating automatic pressuretrol shuts down the burner when the

    A. oil pressure fluctuates due to high oil temperatures
    B. steam pressure fluctuates due to highly acidic feedwater
    C. oil pressure indicator arrow enters *red* or danger zone
    D. predetermined steam pressure setting is reached

33.____

34. The PROPER method for securing lighting globes is to tighten the thumbscrews

    A. hand tight
    B. snug and loosen 1/2 turn
    C. with pliers
    D. till they just support the globe

34.____

35. Persons running an adult program after school hours ask to use the school kitchen to set up a large coffee maker and utensils. Board of Education policy, however, prohibits such use of the kitchen by anyone other than school kitchen workers.
Of the following, it would be MOST appropriate for you to

    A. explain that you are prohibited from doing so and offer an alternative
    B. allow them to use the kitchen if you know them to be responsible and they agree to clean up afterwards
    C. politely inform them that their request does not come under your jurisdiction
    D. allow them to use the kitchen and afterwards have your staff clean up

35.____

36. A damaged or loose spinner cup will cause

    A. high oil pressure
    B. loss of lubricant
    C. low oil pressure
    D. poor atomization of oil

36.____

37. If, during a pay period, one of your employees works 80 hours at the straight time rate of $8.40 per hour and works 16 hours at time and a half, the employee's gross pay for the period is   37.____

    A. $739.20   B. $806.40   C. $873.60   D. $1,008.00

38. The low water cut-off stops the   38.____

    A. boiler on low water
    B. sump pump on low water
    C. sump pump in emergencies
    D. water on low pressure

39. Which of the following chemicals is used to increase alkalinity in feedwater?   39.____

    A. Calcium chloride   B. Sodium chloride
    C. Sodium hydroxide   D. Hydrogen peroxide

40. Which of the following should be used to remove mildew from marble surfaces?   40.____

    A. Bleach   B. Ammonia
    C. Scouring powder   D. Trisodium

———

KEY (CORRECT ANSWERS)

1.	C	11.	A	21.	D	31.	B
2.	B	12.	A	22.	C	32.	C
3.	D	13.	D	23.	A	33.	D
4.	B	14.	B	24.	C	34.	B
5.	A	15.	D	25.	B	35.	A
6.	D	16.	D	26.	A	36.	D
7.	D	17.	D	27.	C	37.	C
8.	B	18.	A	28.	A	38.	A
9.	A	19.	A	29.	A	39.	C
10.	A	20.	B	30.	C	40.	A

———

TEST 2

DIRECTIONS: Each question or incomplete statement is followed by several suggested answers or completions. Select the one that BEST answers the question or completes the statement. *PRINT THE LETTER OF THE CORRECT ANSWER IN THE SPACE AT THE RIGHT.*

1. You have been informed that your building allowance is going to be decreased as part of a city-wide economy drive.
   Of the following, which is the FIRST action you should take in this situation?

   A. Lay-off the worker with the least seniority.
   B. Reduce the amount and complexity of your work in order to absorb the decrease.
   C. Start using less expensive supplies and materials.
   D. Study your custodial operation to determine how best to minimize the effects of the cuts.

   1._____

2. The purpose of the vent line on an oil tank is to allow

   A. water in the oil to evaporate
   B. oil to drain if tank is overfilled
   C. for expansion of the oil as the oil temperature rises
   D. gases to escape into the atmosphere

   2._____

3. A reading of 45° C is indicated on your temperature recorder. This temperature, expressed in degrees Fahrenheit, is

   A. 77   B. 81   C. 113   D. 145

   3._____

4. A dark orange flame in a boiler indicates

   A. low draft
   B. that the refractory is damaged
   C. too much secondary air
   D. too much primary air

   4._____

5. *Metering* faucets

   A. are washerless   B. have aerators
   C. shut off automatically   D. vent air

   5._____

6. You are allowed $72,000 for the operation of your building. Of this amount, your salary is $32,000, your fireman's salary is $25,000, your cleaner earns $10,500, and compensation insurance will cost $750.00.
   After these monies are paid, how much will remain?

   A. $3,150   B. $3,750   C. $4,550   D. $4,570

   6._____

7. It has come to your attention that the police department has one of your cleaners under surveillance.
   Of the following, your action should be to

   A. tell the cleaner that he is under surveillance
   B. tell all your cleaners about the situation and warn them to avoid trouble

   7._____

C.   terminate the cleaner under surveillance
D.   say nothing about the situation to the cleaner

8.   After you prepared a monthly payroll report and sent it to headquarters, you find that you made errors in the report. Of the following, it would be MOST important to

A.   do nothing since a payroll report would be thoroughly checked at headquarters
B.   make all the required changes on the copy you kept
C.   immediately resubmit the report to include the corrected information
D.   adjust the next month's figures to compensate for the error

9.   Stay bolts are found in a boiler's

A.   brick setting   B.   breeching
C.   fire doors   D.   shell

10. A *plumber's friend* is used to

A.   change washers   B.   stop leaks
C.   open corroded fittings   D.   clear stoppages

11. Ballasts are found in

A.   fluorescent fixtures   B.   plumbing fixtures
C.   boiler equalizers   D.   vacuum pumps

12. You hire a person as a cleaner on the recommendation of a friend of yours who is a custodian at another school. When dealing with the newly hired cleaner, it would be MOST appropriate for you to assign

A.   him to the same types of work as you would give to another cleaner with similar abilities
B.   less desirable work to him than you assign to other cleaners in order to avoid giving the impression that he will be receiving special treatment
C.   him work with no regard to his abilities since all workers should be treated the same
D.   him the most desirable work in order to maintain friendship with the custodian who recommended him and to encourage the newly hired cleaner to do good work

13. The size of a boiler tube is based on its

A.   inside diameter   B.   circumference
C.   outside diameter   D.   cross-sectional area

14. Of the following, the LEAST important consideration when preparing a work schedule is the

A.   number of employees on your staff
B.   type of work to be done
C.   age of the employees on your staff
D.   monies budgeted

15. A solenoid valve is also known as a _____ valve.

A.   magnetic oil   B.   thermo-electric
C.   hydraulic   D.   pressure

16. One of your employees earns $8.50 an hour and another employee earns $10.50 an hour. Last week, the employee making $8.50 an hour worked forty hours, and the employee earning $10.50 an hour worked forty-four hours. Assuming that all time in excess of forty hours a week is computed at time and a half, their combined gross pay for the week is

    A. $823.00   B. $840.00   C. $853.00   D. $876.00

16.____

17. Flame failure in a rotary cup oil burner is detected by the

    A. vaporstat   B. aquastat
    C. low draft switch   D. scanner

17.____

18. If the water coming from the faucets in your building is 95°C, it is

    A. warm   B. too hot
    C. tepid   D. too cold

18.____

19. You are writing a memorandum to your supervisor concerning problems you have been having with certain boiler room equipment.
Of the following, it would be MOST important for your memorandum to

    A. be long and include proper terminology to let your supervisor know you are technically competent and knowledgeable about proper boiler plant operation
    B. explain the problem clearly and to provide possible solutions
    C. explain the problem in such a way as to avoid giving the impression that the problems are your fault or that you did not do enough to minimize the effects
    D. be respectful in tone and grammatically correct

19.____

20. One of the classrooms in your building is often littered with paper, other trash, and in otherwise unacceptable condition at the end of the day.
Of the following, it would be MOST appropriate for you to

    A. tell the children that they are to leave the room as clean at the end of the day as they find it in the morning
    B. speak to the principal about the room's condition in order to obtain her assistance to resolve the situation
    C. advise the teacher that you will instruct your cleaners not to clean the room unless he cooperates in keeping it clean
    D. regularly check the room to determine which of the children are responsible for its condition

20.____

21. One of your employees has a gross bi-weekly salary of $600 and a FICA deduction of 5%.
His FICA deduction for a period of 4 weeks is

    A. $3   B. $6   C. $30   D. $60

21.____

22. A(n) _____ has a gauge glass.

    A. pressure gauge   B. inspection window
    C. condensate tank   D. transom

22.____

23. One standard square of roofing shingle will cover square feet.

    A. 1   B. 10   C. 100   D. 144

23.____

24. _____ NOT a part of low pressure boilers.   24.____

    A. Crown sheets   B. Impellers
    C. Weep holes   D. Stay rods

25. If one person is normally assigned to a facility for every 33,000 square feet and you have   25.____
82,000 square feet, your manpower requirement is

    A. 1   B. 1 1/2   C. 2   D. 2 1/2

26. Your cleaning crew's morale is very low because the school is often vandalized, making   26.____
it very difficult for your workers to maintain the building properly.
Of the following, it would be MOST appropriate for you to tell your crew

    A. that you are aware of the effort they put in even though the building does not reflect
        the work they do
    B. not to work so hard because their work is not appreciated and it is a losing battle
    C. that they get paid for their work and, therefore, there is no justification for their low
        morale
    D. not to concern themselves about vandalism since it is a social problem, not a cus-
        todial matter

27. Nematodes are   27.____

    A. weeds   B. elevator fuses
    C. electrical circuits   D. lawn pests

28. A *supervisory* circuit is found in   28.____

    A. boiler controls   B. the principal's intercom
    C. hot water tanks   D. fire alarms

29. Braided packing is found in   29.____

    A. electrical insulation   B. stuffing boxes
    C. wall insulation   D. junction boxes

30. The gas meter in your building reads 1234 on the 1st of the month and 1356 at the end   30.____
of the month.
If the meter has a multiplier of 60, how much gas was consumed for the month?

    A. 813.60   B. 4260   C. 7320   D. 81360

31. Which of the following is NOT used to control boiler water level?   31.____
A

    A. condensate return pump   B. vacuum pump
    C. blow down valve   D. feedwater regulator

32. A water-charged fire extinguisher should NOT be used on a(n) _____ fire.   32.____

    A. paper   B. oil   C. wood   D. trash

33. A *pope's head* is used to clean   33.____

    A. floors   B. boiler tubes
    C. windows   D. sidewalks

34. The drain in your school yard is stopped up after each rainfall.
Which one of the following is the MOST appropriate action to take to correct this situation?

    A. Remove the strainer basket
    B. Schedule regular drain cleaning
    C. Blank off grating
    D. Have the drain *snaked* on an annual basis

34._____

35. Of the following, which is the LARGEST size of coal?

    A. Rice   B. Buckwheat   C. Pea   D. Walnut

35._____

36. To perform a low water cut-off test, you should

    A. shut off the water at the tempering valve
    B. open the bypass valve on the feedwater regulator
    C. shut down the water supply until the boiler shuts off
    D. open the pressure relief valve

36._____

37. A recently hired cleaner does not complete tasks within the time periods that you believe to be proper for his work.
Of the following, the FIRST action you should take is to

    A. warn him that his job may be in jeopardy if he does not improve
    B. avoid mentioning anything about his work for the first few weeks of his employment in order to give him time to learn what is expected from him
    C. ask other employees to encourage him to work harder and faster
    D. observe him while he works to determine the reasons he takes so long to complete this work

37._____

38. This year, the fuel consumption at your school has significantly increased over last year's consumption even though the weather for both years has been quite similar. You are checking your heating system to determine the reason for the increase.
Which of the following is LEAST likely to be the reason for the higher consumption?

    A. Dirty fire tubes
    B. Leaking steam traps
    C. High flue gas temperature
    D. High steam temperature

38._____

39. A teacher tells you that one of your cleaners broke her classroom movie projector. She states that when she left the room at the end of the preceding school day, the cleaner was working in her room and the projector was operating fine. The next morning it wasn't working.
For this situation, you should FIRST

    A. accuse the cleaner of breaking it to test his reaction
    B. order the cleaner to talk to the teacher to get the matter resolved
    C. question the cleaner to find out what, if anything, he knows about this situation
    D. watch the cleaner for several days to see if he does anything to indicate guilt

39._____

40. Of the following, which is the MOST likely indication of soot build-up in boiler tubes?   40.____

    A. A high CO_2 reading
    B. A high furnace draft reading
    C. High boiler pressure
    D. High stack temperature

_____

KEY (CORRECT ANSWERS)

1.	D	11.	A	21.	D	31.	B
2.	D	12.	A	22.	C	32.	B
3.	C	13.	C	23.	C	33.	C
4.	A	14.	C	24.	B	34.	B
5.	C	15.	A	25.	D	35.	C
6.	B	16.	A	26.	A	36.	C
7.	D	17.	D	27.	D	37.	D
8.	C	18.	B	28.	D	38.	D
9.	D	19.	B	29.	B	39.	C
10.	D	20.	B	30.	C	40.	D

_____

EXAMINATION SECTION
TEST 1

DIRECTIONS: Each question or incomplete statement is followed by several suggested answers or completions. Select the one that BEST answers the question or completes the statement. *PRINT THE LETTER OF THE CORRECT ANSWER IN THE SPACE AT THE RIGHT.*

1. The BEST of the following substances in which to store used paint brushes is   1._____

    A. gasoline   B. mineral oil
    C. alcohol   D. linseed oil

2. A CORRECT statement with respect to the use of a file is: 2._____

    A. The coarser the tooth of a file, the less metal will be removed on each stroke of the file
    B. Files are generally made to cut in one direction only
    C. When a file is used to pry apart materials, light pressure should be maintained
    D. In filing rounded surfaces, the file should rest on the work at all times

3. An ACCEPTABLE material to use on a door to overcome slight sticking to the door jamb is   3._____

    A. tallow candle   B. graphite
    C. mineral oil   D. #6 oil

4. The PROPER type of wrench to use on plated or polished pipe is a(n) _____ wrench.   4._____

    A. monkey   B. pipe   C. open end   D. strap

5. Of the following, the room which requires the GREATEST amount of illumination per square foot is the   5._____

    A. library   B. gymnasium
    C. auditorium   D. sewing room

6. If one of the electric bulbs in a classroom fails to light up when the switch is snapped, the trouble is MOST likely with the   6._____

    A. switch   B. wiring   C. fuse   D. bulb

7. In general, wood should be fine sanded _____ the grain.   7._____

    A. across   B. diagonal to
    C. with   D. circular to

8. The reason for blowing down the water column of a boiler daily is to   8._____

    A. prevent priming or foaming in the boiler
    B. keep the passages above and below the glass clean
    C. remove lime and other mineral matter from boiler feedwater
    D. reduce the possibility of excess steam pressure from building up

9. A CORRECT step in the procedure of blowing down a low pressure boiler is: 9.____

    A. Close return valves before starting to open the blow-off valve
    B. Start the job while the boiler is in operation
    C. Add fresh water rapidly to reach the maximum level
    D. Close blow-off valve when the water reaches the lowest row of tubes

10. To determine if efficient burning of fuel is occurring, the device which is used is a(n)   10.____

    A. orsat apparatus   B. thermostat
    C. pyrometer   D. bourdon tube

11. The PROPER tool to use to break up clinkers sticking to the grate is a   11.____

    A. shovel   B. slice bar
    C. grate bar   D. rake

12. One of the possible results of closing ash pit doors to regulate draft is   12.____

    A. warping or melting of grates
    B. reduced formation of clinkers
    C. steam will become superheated
    D. live coals will fall into the ash pit

13. Good firing methods require that   13.____

    A. the firebed be thick enough to prevent air from passing through
    B. each side of the grate be kept bare to allow cool air to reach the stack
    C. live coals should not be allowed to burn beneath the grates
    D. the fire be stirred every hour to reduce the amount of unburned gases

14. Of the following, the one that is CORRECT with respect to the burning of hard coal is: 14.____

    A. To prevent clinkers, a hard coal fire should never be poked
    B. The fire bed should not be more than 6 inches thick at any time
    C. Air holes in the bed should be made with a rake or slice bar
    D. Infrequent heavy firing will reduce the possibility of forming holes

15. The MAIN purpose of a Hartford Loop as a return connection for a steam boiler is to   15.____

    A. remove air from the return lines
    B. prevent a boiler from losing its water
    C. allow reduction in boiler header size
    D. reduce friction in return lines

16. If a boiler fails to deliver enough heat, the MOST probable of the following reasons is the   16.____

    A. leaking of the boiler manhole
    B. boiler operating at excessive output
    C. heating surface is covered with soot
    D. unsteady water line as shown by the gauge glass

17. Generally, thermostatic traps of radiators are used to   17.____

    A. prevent the flow of water and air and allow the passage of steam
    B. prevent the passage of steam and allow the passage of water and air

C.   stop air from entering the radiator to prevent it from becoming air-bound
D.   relieve the radiator of excess steam if pressure rises too high

18.   When a heating boiler is in operation, the safety valve should be tested   18._____

A.   semi-annually
B.   weekly
C.   monthly
D.   whenever it seems to be stuck

19.   In the horizontal rotary cup oil burner, the MAIN purpose of the rotary cup is to   19._____

A.   provide air for ignition of the oil
B.   pump oil into the burner
C.   atomize the oil into small drops
D.   turn the flame in a circle to heat the furnace walls evenly

20.   The BEST reason for having gaskets on manholes of a boiler is to   20._____

A.   prevent leakage from the boiler
B.   provide emergency exit for excessive steam pressure
C.   provide easy access to the boiler for cleaning
D.   prevent corrosion at manholes

21.   The MAIN purpose of expansion joints in steam lines is to   21._____

A.   provide for changes in length of heated pipe
B.   allow for connection of additional radiators
C.   provide locations for valves
D.   reduce breakage of pipe due to minor movement in the building

22.   If too much water is put in a boiler, the result will be   22._____

A.   excessive smoke
B.   excessive rate of steam output
C.   excessive fuel consumption
D.   unsteady water line

23.   Piping that carries condensate and air from radiators of a heating system is called   23._____

A.   dry return if above boiler water line
B.   drip line
C.   wet return if above boiler water line
D.   riser runout

24.   Suppose a boiler smokes through the fire door.   24._____
      Of the following, the LEAST likely cause is

A.   dirty or clogged flues
B.   inferior fuel
C.   defective chimney draft
D.   air leaks into boiler

25. Of the following, the statement concerning accident prevention that is NOT correct is: 25.____

    A. Ladders should be unpainted
    B. Remove finger rings before beginning to mop
    C. Wear loose-fitting clothes when working around boilers or machinery
    D. Set ladder bottom at about 1/5 the ladder length away from the wall against which the ladder rests

_____

KEY (CORRECT ANSWERS)

1.	D	11.	B
2.	B	12.	A
3.	A	13.	C
4.	D	14.	A
5.	D	15.	B
6.	D	16.	C
7.	C	17.	B
8.	B	18.	B
9.	B	19.	C
10.	A	20.	A

21.	A
22.	C
23.	A
24.	D
25.	C

_____

TEST 2

DIRECTIONS: Each question or incomplete statement is followed by several suggested answers or completions. Select the one that BEST answers the question or completes the statement. *PRINT THE LETTER OF THE CORRECT ANSWER IN THE SPACE AT THE RIGHT.*

1. When the oil burner reset button is pressed, the burner motor does not start. The FIRST thing to check is the

    A. oil supply in oil tanks
    B. possibility of a blown fuse
    C. oil strainers which may be clogged
    D. dirty stack switch

    1._____

2. When a heating plant is laid up for the summer, one of the steps the fireman should take with respect to the boiler is to tap the brace and stay rods with a hammer. The MAIN reason for this is to

    A. clean these parts of accumulated rust and dirt
    B. make certain these parts are in place and not out of line
    C. remove them for storage during summer and early autumn seasons
    D. make certain they are tight and not broken

    2._____

3. In the event of a bomb threat, the custodian should take the precaution to

    A. open ash pit and fire doors of boilers
    B. pull the main switch to cut off all power in the building
    C. operate with the least number of water services possible
    D. empty water from boilers immediately after covering fire with ashes

    3._____

4. The type of fire extinguisher that requires protection against freezing is

    A. carbon dioxide
    B. carbon tetrachloride (pyrene)
    C. soda acid
    D. calcium chloride

    4._____

5. A CORRECT procedure in recharging soda acid fire extinguishers is:

    A. The soda charge should be completed dissolved in 28 gallons of boiling water
    B. The filled acid bottle should be tightly stoppered before it is placed back in the extinguisher
    C. The extinguisher must be recharged after use regardless of extent of use
    D. Be sure to fill container with soda solution to the top of container up to threads of cap

    5._____

6. The MOST common cause of slipperiness of a terrazzo floor after being washed is the

    A. failure to rinse floor clean after cleaning agent is used
    B. destruction of floor seal by cleaning agent
    C. incomplete removal of dirt from the floor
    D. use of oil in the cleaning process

    6._____

7. When electric lighting fixtures are washed, a precaution to observe is that   7.___

   A. the metal part of the fixture should be washed with a warm mild ammonia solution
   B. the holding screws of glass globes should be loosened about half a turn after cleaning globes
   C. trisodium phosphate should not be used in washing glass globes because it dulls glass
   D. chain links of fixture should be loosened to enable removal of entire fixture

8. Inside burns on recently cut pipe are USUALLY removed by   8.___

   A. filing   B. turning   C. reaming   D. sanding

9. When the average temperature for a day is 48°F, the number of degree days for that day is   9.___

   A. 22   B. 27   C. 12   D. 17

10. Water hammer will MOST likely occur in the   10.___

   A. self-closing valves of a drinking fountain
   B. bends in a pipe line where air can accumulate
   C. globe valve on the supply line to a fixture
   D. angle valve on the steam supply line to a radiator

11. To remove a stoppage in a trap which has not cleared by the use of a force cup, the tool to use is a(n)   11.___

   A. yarning tool   B. auger
   C. expansion bit   D. trowel

12. If the float of a flush tank leaks and fills with water, the MOST probable result will be   12.___

   A. no water in the tank
   B. ball cock remains open
   C. water will flow over the tank rim
   D. flush ball will not seat properly

13. Fresh air inlets are GENERALLY installed in connection with a   13.___

   A. house trap   B. roof vent
   C. sump pump   D. branch soil pipe

14. The PRIMARY function of the water trap in the waste line from a wash bowl is to   14.___

   A. hold excess water from flooding waste line
   B. prevent the flow of sewer gas into the room
   C. catch particles and refuse that may enter the line with the water
   D. provide an easy means for cleaning and repairing the waste line

15. The BEST lubricant for a cylinder lock is   15.___

   A. crude oil   B. machine oil
   C. tallow   D. graphite

16. A window sash holds the   16.___

   A. casing   B. glass   C. jambs   D. sills

17. The BEST procedure to follow to determine the actual cleaning ability of a specific material is to

    A. test its performance
    B. read the specifications
    C. ask the manufacturer
    D. examine trade literature

17._____

Questions 18-21.

DIRECTIONS: Questions 18 through 21 are to be answered on the basis of the following occurrence.

An accident occured at P.S. 947 on Monday, January 14, resulting in the injury of a fireman-cleaner named John Jones. Jones was found unconscious on the floor of the boiler room. He showed evidence of a head injury. An ambulance was called immediately. Jones was treated by the ambulance attendant, who found no serious injury and treated the head wound. Jones, when asked about the cause of the injury, stated that he had fallen over a coal shovel lying in his path. The head injury apparently resulted from the hard contact of Jones' head with a concrete post. Jones was then taken home and was advised to check with a doctor if he felt groggy or ill. An examination of the boiler room revealed that an electric light located near the scene of the accident was out and that the area was quite dark. There were no witnesses to the accident.

18. Of the following, the information MOST necessary to make the required report on the accident is

    A. Jones' age
    B. Jones' work habits
    C. the name of the person who found Jones injured
    D. whether Jones was covered by Workmen's Compensation

18._____

19. When Jones was found, a safety precaution that should have been taken was

    A. extinguishing the fire in the furnace
    B. the removal of Jones to a place where the lighting was more satisfactory
    C. avoiding movement of Jones to prevent further injury
    D. raising Jones' head to restore him to consciousness

19._____

20. In accordance with Worker's Compensation regulations, Jones has the right to

    A. compensation if his injuries keep him from work more than one week
    B. use any doctor provided the doctor is approved by the custodian
    C. compensation greater than the amount of his wages if he is seriously injured
    D. compensation only if he proves he did not place the shovel where it was found

20._____

21. The MOST important lesson that the custodian should learn from this accident is that

    A. before an employee starts work, his place of work should be inspected by the custodian
    B. even experienced firemen-cleaners require regular weekly training in the proper performance of their duties

21._____

C. employees should be required to turn in old burned out electric bulbs before receiving new ones
D. regular inspections of work spaces are required to reduce accidents to a minimum

22. Information which is of the LEAST value in a report of unlawful entry into a school building is the

    A. estimated value of missing property
    B. means of entry
    C. time and date of entry
    D. general description of the school building

22._____

23. You notice several children marking an entrance door with chalk.
The MOST desirable immediate action to take is to

    A. stop the children and tell them not to do this again
    B. ask the principal to stop the children from defacing the door
    C. take the names of the children and write to their parents
    D. remove the chalk marks, but say nothing to the children

23._____

24. Suppose that the principal advises you that there are peddlers selling their wares at sidewalk locations surrounding the school premises.
The MOST appropriate action to take first is to

    A. put up signs warning the peddlers that they are violating the law
    B. advise the peddlers that such activity on sidewalks of the school is illegal and to move on
    C. call the police immediately to clear the sidewalks
    D. suggest that the teachers tell their pupils not to patronize these unsupervised peddlers

24._____

25. A parent complains that her child refuses to use the school toilet because it is unclean.
The FIRST step you should take upon receipt of the complaint from the school principal is to

    A. advise the principal that the toilets are kept clean and that the complaint is unwarranted
    B. tell the cleaner in charge of the floor on which the toilet is located to clean the toilet properly
    C. visit the school toilets to check on the statements made in the complaint
    D. ask the parent to see the toilets for herself rather than take the word of her child

25._____

KEY (CORRECT ANSWERS)

1.	B		11.	B
2.	D		12.	B
3.	C		13.	A
4.	C		14.	B
5.	C		15.	D
6.	A		16.	B
7.	B		17.	A
8.	C		18.	C
9.	D		19.	C
10.	A		20.	A

21.	D
22.	D
23.	A
24.	B
25.	C

———

EXAMINATION SECTION
TEST 1

DIRECTIONS: Each question or incomplete statement is followed by several suggested
answers or completions. Select the one that BEST answers the question or
completes the statement. *PRINT THE LETTER OF THE CORRECT ANSWER
IN THE SPACE AT THE RIGHT.*

1. Of the following daily jobs in the schedule of a custodian, the one he should do FIRST in   1._____
the morning is to

    A.   hang out the flag
    B.   open all doors of the school
    C.   fire the boilers
    D.   dust the principal's office

2. When a school custodian is newly assigned to a building at the start of the school term,   2._____
his FIRST step should be to

    A.   examine the building to determine needed maintenance and repair
    B.   meet the principal and discuss plans for operation and maintenance of the building
    C.   call a meeting of the teaching and custodial staff to explain his plans for the build-
ing
    D.   review the records of maintenance and operation left by the previous custodian

3. A detergent is a material GENERALLY used for   3._____

    A.   coating floors to resist water
    B.   snow removal
    C.   insulation of steam and hot water lines
    D.   cleaning purposes

4. A good disinfectant is one that will   4._____

    A.   have a clean odor which will cover up disagreeable odors
    B.   destroy germs and create more sanitary conditions
    C.   dissolve encrusted dirt and other sources of disagreeable odors
    D.   dissolve grease and other materials that may cause stoppage in toilet waste lines

5. To help prevent leaks at the joints of water lines, the pipe threads are commonly covered   5._____
with

    A.   tar   B.   cup grease
    C.   rubber cement   D.   white lead

6. The advantage of using screws instead of nails is that   6._____

    A.   they have greater holding power
    B.   they are available in a greater variety than are nails
    C.   a hammer is not required for joining wood members
    D.   they are less expensive

7. Of the following, the grade of steel wool that is FINEST is   7._____

    A.   00   B.   0   C.   1   D.   2

8. The material used with solder to make it stick better is   8.____

    A. oakum   B. lye   C. oil   D. flux

9. In using a floor brush in a corridor, a cleaner should be instructed to   9.____

    A. use moderately long pull strokes whenever possible
    B. make certain that there is no overlap on sweeping strokes
    C. give the brush a slight jerk after each stroke to free it of loose dirt
    D. keep the sweeping surface of the brush firmly flat on the floor to obtain maximum coverage

10. Of the following, the MOST proper procedure in sweeping classroom floors is to   10.____

    A. open all windows before beginning the sweeping operation
    B. move forward while sweeping
    C. alternate pull and push strokes
    D. sweep under desks on both sides of an aisle while moving down the aisle

11. PROPER care of floor brushes includes   11.____

    A. washing brushes daily after each use with warm soap solution
    B. dipping brushes in kerosene periodically to remove dirt
    C. washing with warm soap solution at least once a month
    D. avoiding contact with soap or soda solutions to prevent drying of bristles

12. An advantage of vacuum cleaning rather than sweeping a floor with a floor brush is that   12.____

    A. stationary furniture will not be touched by the cleaning tool
    B. the problem of dust on furniture is reduced
    C. the initial cost of the apparatus is less than the cost of an equivalent number of floor brushes
    D. daily sweeping of rooms and corridors can be eliminated

13. Sweeping compound for use on rubber tile, asphalt tile or sealed wood floors must NOT contain   13.____

    A. sawdust   B. water
    C. oil soap   D. floor oil

14. Of the following, the MOST desirable material to use in dusting furniture is a   14.____

    A. soft cotton cloth   B. hand towel
    C. counter brush   D. feather duster

15. In high dusting of walls and ceilings, the CORRECT procedure is to   15.____

    A. begin with the lower walls and proceed up to the ceiling
    B. remove pictures and window shades only if they are dusty
    C. clean the windows thoroughly before dusting any other part of the room
    D. begin with the ceiling and then dust the walls

16. When cleaning a classroom, the cleaner should   16.____

    A. dust desks before sweeping
    B. dust desks after sweeping

C.   open windows during the desk dusting process
D.   begin dusting at rows most distant from the entrance door

17.   Too much water on asphalt tile is objectionable MAINLY because the tile   17._____

A.   will tend to become discolored or spotted
B.   may be loosened from the floor
C.   will be softened and made uneven
D.   colors will tend to run

18.   To reduce the slip hazard resulting from waxing linoleum, the MOST practical of the fol-   18._____
lowing methods is to

A.   apply the wax in one heavy coat
B.   apply the wax after varnishing the linoleum
C.   buff the wax surface thoroughly
D.   apply the wax in several thin coats

19.   Assume that the water-emulsion wax needed for routine waxing in your building is 15 gal-   19._____
lons per month. This wax is supplied in 55 gallon drums.
To cover your needs for a year, the MINIMUM number of drums you would have to
request is

A.   two   B.   three   C.   four   D.   six

20.   In washing down walls, the correct procedure is to start at the bottom of the wall and   20._____
work to the top.
The MOST important reason for this is that

A.   dirt streaking will tend to be avoided or easily removed
B.   less cleansing agent will be required
C.   rinse water will not be required
D.   the time for cleaning the wall is less than if washing started at the top of the wall

21.   In mopping a wood floor of a classroom, the cleaner should   21._____

A.   mop against the grain of the wood wherever possible
B.   mop as large an area as possible at one time
C.   wet the floor before mopping with a cleaning agent
D.   mop only aisles and clear areas and use a scrub brush under desks and chairs

22.   A precaution to observe in mopping asphalt tile floors is: 22._____

A.   Keep all pails off such floors because they will leave water marks
B.   Do not wear rubber footwear while mopping those floors
C.   Use circular motion in rinsing and drying the floor to avoid streaking
D.   Never use a cleaning agent containing trisodium phosphate

23.   The MOST commonly used cleansing agent for the removal of ink stains from a wood   23._____
floor is

A.   kerosene   B.   oxalic acid
C.   lye   D.   bicarbonate soda

24. The FIRST operation in routine cleaning of toilets and washrooms is to 　　24.____

    A. wash floors
    B. clean walls
    C. clean washbasins
    D. empty waste receptacles

25. To eliminate the cause of odors in toilet rooms, the tile floors should be mopped with 　　25.____

    A. a mild solution of soap and trisodium phosphate in water
    B. dilute lye solution followed by a hot water rinse
    C. dilute muriatic acid dissolved in hot water
    D. carbon tetrachloride dissolved in hot water

———

KEY (CORRECT ANSWERS)

1.	C	11.	C
2.	B	12.	B
3.	D	13.	D
4.	B	14.	A
5.	D	15.	D
6.	A	16.	B
7.	A	17.	B
8.	D	18.	D
9.	C	19.	C
10.	B	20.	A

21.	C
22.	A
23.	B
24.	D
25.	A

———

TEST 2

DIRECTIONS: Each question or incomplete statement is followed by several suggested answers or completions. Select the one that BEST answers the question or completes the statement. *PRINT THE LETTER OF THE CORRECT ANSWER IN THE SPACE AT THE RIGHT.*

1. The PRINCIPAL reason why soap should NOT be used in cleaning windows is that   1._____

    A. it causes loosening of the putty
    B. it may cause rotting of the wood frame
    C. a film is left on the window, requiring additional rinsing
    D. frequent use of soap will cause the glass to become permanently clouded

2. The CHIEF value of having windows consisting of many small panes of glass is that   2._____

    A. the window is much stronger
    B. accident hazards are eliminated
    C. the cost of replacing broken panes is low
    D. cleaning windows consisting of small panes is easier than cleaning a window with a large undivided pane

3. Cleansing powders such as Ajax should NOT be used to clean and polish brass MAINLY because   3._____

    A. the brass turns a much darker color
    B. such cleansers have no effect on tarnish
    C. the surface of the brass may become scratched
    D. too much fine dust is raised in the polishing process

4. To remove chalk marks on sidewalks and cemented playground areas, the MOST acceptable cleaning method is   4._____

    A. using a brush with warm water
    B. using a brush with warm water containing some kerosene
    C. hosing down such areas with water
    D. using a brush with a solution of muriatic acid in water

5. The MOST important reason for oiling wood floors is that   5._____

    A. it keeps the dust from rising during the sweeping process
    B. the need for daily sweeping of classroom floors is eliminated
    C. oiled floors present a better appearance than waxed floors
    D. the wood surface will become waterproof and stain-proof

6. After oil has been sprayed on a wood floor, the sprayer should be cleaned before storing it.   6._____
The USUAL cleaning material for this purpose is

    A. ammonia water   B. salt
    C. kerosene   D. alcohol

7. The *MOST* desirable agent for routine cleaning of slate blackboards is   7.____

    A. warm water containing trisodium phosphate
    B. mild soap solution in warm water
    C. kerosene in warm water
    D. warm water alone

8. Neatsfoot oil is commonly used to   8.____

    A. oil light machinery
    B. prepare compound
    C. clean metal fixtures
    D. treat leather-covered chairs

Questions 9-12.

DIRECTIONS: Column I lists cleaning agents used by a custodian. Cleaning operations are given in Column II. Select the MOST common cleaning operation for the cleaning agents listed in Column I and print the letter representing your choice next to the number of the agent in the space at the right.

COLUMN I

  9. Ammonia

10. Muriatic acid

11. Carbon tetrachloride

12. Trisodium phosphate

COLUMN II

A. Add to water to clean marble walls   9.____

B. Remove chewing gum from wood floors   10.____

C. Wash down calcimined ceilings   11.____

D. Add to water for washing rubber tile floors   12.____

E. Remove rust stains from porcelain

F. Cleaning brass

13. In order to stop a faucet from dripping, the custodian would USUALLY have to replace the   13.____

    A. cap nut   B. seat   C. washer   D. spindle

14. Drinking fountains should be adjusted so that the height of the water stream is about _____ inches.   14.____

    A. 6   B. 3   C. 0   D. 12

15. Before starting up the boilers each morning, the custodian or fireman should make certain that   15.____

    A. all blow-off cocks and valves are open
    B. the water is at a safe level
    C. radiator and univent valves are open
    D. the main smoke damper is fully closed

16. If the radiator on a one-pipe heating system rattles or makes noise, the PROBABLE   16._____
cause is that the

    A.   steam pressure is too high
    B.   steam pressure is too low
    C.   steam valve is wide open
    D.   radiator is air-bound

17. Of the following, the LARGEST size of hard coal is   17._____

    A.   chestnut   B.   egg   C.   stove   D.   pea

18. The MAIN purpose of baffle plates in a furnace is to   18._____

    A.   change the direction of flow of heated gases
    B.   retard the burning of gases
    C.   increase the combustion ratio of the fuel
    D.   prevent the escape of flue gases through furnace openings

19. The MAIN difference between a steam header and a steam riser for a given heating sys-   19._____
tem is that the

    A.   riser is usually larger than the header
    B.   header is larger than the riser
    C.   riser is a horizontal line and the header is a vertical line
    D.   header is insulated while the riser is not insulated

20. The try-cocks of steam boilers are used to   20._____

    A.   act as safety valves
    B.   empty the boiler of water
    C.   test steam pressure in the boiler
    D.   find the height of water in the boiler

21. The MOST important reason for cleaning soot from a boiler is that   21._____

    A.   soot blocks the passage of steam from the boiler
    B.   soot gets into the boiler room and makes it dirty
    C.   soot reduces the heating efficiency of a boiler
    D.   the pressure of soot is a frequent cause of the cracking of boiler tubes

22. Panic bolts are standard equipment in school buildings.   22._____
Their MAIN purpose is to

    A.   reduce unauthorized opening of doors and closets
    B.   allow for easy opening of exit doors of the building
    C.   permit rapid removal of screens from windows when a fire occurs
    D.   shut storeroom doors automatically to reduce fire hazard

23. The term RPM is GENERALLY used in connection with the   23._____

    A.   speed of ventilating fans
    B.   water capacity of pipe
    C.   heating quality of fuel
    D.   electrical output of a transformer

24. A hacksaw is a light-framed saw MOST commonly used to

    A. cut curved patterns in metal
    B. trim edges
    C. cut wood in confined spaces
    D. cut metal

24.____

25. A kilowatt is equivalent to _____ watts.

    A. 500   B. 2,000   C. 1,500   D. 1,000

25.____

_____

KEY (CORRECT ANSWERS)

1.	C		11.	B
2.	C		12.	D
3.	C		13.	C
4.	A		14.	B
5.	A		15.	B
6.	C		16.	D
7.	D		17:	B
8.	D		18.	A
9.	A		19.	B
10.	E		20.	D

21.	C
22.	B
23.	A
24.	D
25.	D

_____

EXAMINATION SECTION
TEST 1

DIRECTIONS: Each question or incomplete statement is followed by several suggested answers or completions. Select the one that BEST answers the question or completes the statement. *PRINT THE LETTER OF THE CORRECT ANSWER IN THE SPACE AT THE RIGHT.*

1. Of the following, the BEST way for you to make sure that a cleaner understands a spoken order which you have given to him is for you to   1._____

    A. ask him to repeat the order in his own words
    B. ask him whether he has understood the order
    C. watch how he begins to follow the order
    D. ask him whether he has any questions about the order

2. You have called a meeting with your cleaners to get their suggestions on ways to keep up   2._____
cleaning standards in spite of budget cutbacks.
You will MOST likely be successful in encouraging them to participate in the discussion if you

    A. start the meeting by giving the cleaners all your own suggestions first
    B. keep the meeting going by talking whenever the cleaners have nothing to say
    C. get the cleaners to *think out loud* by asking them for their interpretations of the problem
    D. comment on and evaluate the suggestions made by each cleaner immediately after he makes them

3. If a custodian knows that rumors being spread by his assistants are false, he should   3._____

    A. tell the assistants that the rumors are false
    B. tell the assistants the facts which the rumors have falsified
    C. threaten to discipline any assistant who spreads the rumors
    D. find out which assistant started the rumor and have him suspended

4. One of your cleaners tells you in private that he wants to quit his job.   4._____
The FIRST thing you should do in handling this matter is to

    A. ask the cleaner why he wants to quit his job
    B. tell the cleaner to take a few days to think it over
    C. refer the cleaner to the personnel office
    D. try to convince the cleaner not to quit his job

5. The MOST important reason why a custodian should seek the suggestions of his cleaners on job-related matters is that the   5._____

    A. cleaners generally have greater knowledge of job-related matters than the custodian
    B. cleaners will tend to have a greater feeling of participation in their jobs by making suggestions
    C. custodians will be able to hold the cleaners responsible for any suggestions he follows
    D. custodians can win the respect of his cleaners by showing them the errors in their suggestions

6. Your supervisor has ordered you to announce to your cleaners a new cleaning rule with which you disagree. You should

    A. admit honestly to your cleaners that you disagree with the rule
    B. announce the rule to your cleaners without expressing your disagreement
    C. encourage your cleaners by telling them you agree with the rule
    D. tell your supervisor that you refuse to announce any rule with which you disagree

6._____

7. Of the following, the BEST practice to follow in criticizing the work performance of a cleaner is to

    A. save up several criticisms and make them all at one time
    B. soften your criticism by being humorous
    C. have another cleaner, who has more seniority, give the criticism
    D. make sure that you explain to the cleaner the reasons for your criticisms

7._____

8. Of the following, the BEST way to reduce unnecessary absences among your cleaners is to

    A. ask your cleaners the reason for their absence every time they are absent
    B. rely entirely on written warnings once every month to cleaners who have been absent too often during the month
    C. have your cleaners make a formal written report to you every time they are absent, explaining the reason for their absence
    D. threaten to fire your cleaners every time they are absent

8._____

9. A group of students complains to you about the lack of cleanliness in your building. You realize that budget cutbacks have unavoidably led to shortages in manpower and equipment for the cleaning staff.
Of the following, the BEST way for you to answer these students is to

    A. tell them frankly that the cleanliness of the building is none of their business as students
    B. apologize for the condition of the building and promise that your men will work harder
    C. tell them to take their complaints to the administration and not to you
    D. explain the reasons for the building's condition and what you are doing to improve it

9._____

10. The MOST important role of the school custodian in promoting public relations in the community should be to help

    A. increase understanding between the custodial staff and the community which it serves
    B. keep from community attention any failings on the part of the custodial staff
    C. increase the authority of the custodial staff over the community with which it deals
    D. keep the community from interfering in the operations of the custodial staff

10._____

11. A teacher conducting a class calls you to complain that the cleaners cleaning the empty classroom next to hers are being unnecessarily noisy.
Of the following, the BEST response to the teacher is to tell her that

11._____

A. she should go next door to tell the cleaners to stop the unnecessary noise
B. you will tell the cleaners about her complaint and instruct them not to make unnecessary noise
C. she should file a formal complaint against the cleaners with your superior
D. you will come to her classroom to judge for yourself whether the cleaners are being unnecessarily noisy

12. The attitude a school custodian should generally maintain toward the faculty and students is one of   12._____

    A. avoidance   B. superiority
    C. courtesy   D. servility

13. The flow of oil in an automatic rotary cup oil burner is regulated by a(n)   13._____

    A. thermostat   B. metering valve
    C. pressure relief valve   D. electric eye

14. The one of the following devices that is required on both coal-fired and oil-fired boilers is a(n)   14._____

    A. safety valve
    B. low water cut-off
    C. feedwater regulator
    D. electrostatic precipitator

15. The type of fuel which must be preheated before it can be burned efficiently is   15._____

    A. natural gas   B. pea coal
    C. number 2 oil   D. number 6 oil

16. A suction gauge in a fuel-oil transfer system is USUALLY located   16._____

    A. before the strainer
    B. after the strainer and before the pump
    C. after the pump and before the pressure relief valve
    D. after the pressure relief valve

17. The FIRST item that should be checked before starting the fire in a steam boiler is the   17._____

    A. thermostat   B. vacuum pump
    C. boiler water level   D. feedwater regulator

18. Operation of a boiler that has been *sealed* by the Department of Buildings is   18._____

    A. prohibited
    B. permitted when the outside temperature is below 32° F
    C. permitted between the hours of 6:00 A.M. and 8:00 A.M. and 9:00 P.M. and 11:00 P.M.
    D. permitted only for the purpose of heating domestic water

19. Lowering the thermostat setting by 5 degrees during the heating season will result in fuel savings of MOST NEARLY _____ percent.   19._____

    A. 2   B. 5   C. 20   D. 50

20. An electrically-driven rotary fuel oil pump MUST be protected from internal damage by   20.____
the installation in the oil line of a

    A. discharge side strainer   B. check valve
    C. suction gauge   D. pressure relief valve

21. A float-thermostatic steam trap in a condensate return line that is operating properly will   21.____
allow

    A. steam and air to pass and will hold back condensate
    B. air and condensate to pass and will hold back steam
    C. steam and condensate to pass and will hold back air
    D. steam to pass and will hold back air and condensate

22. Changes in the combustion efficiency of a boiler can be determined by comparing   22.____
changes in stack temperature and

    A. steam pressure in the header
    B. over the fire draft
    C. percentage of carbon dioxide
    D. equivalent of direct radiation

23. The classification of the coal that is USUALLY burned in a city school building is   23.____

    A. anthracite   B. bituminous
    C. semi-bituminous   D. lignite

24. A boiler is equipped with the following pressuretrols: 24.____
       I. Manual-reset
      II. Modulating
     III. High-limit
The CORRECT sequence in which these devices should be actuated by rising steam
pressure is

    A. I, II, III   B. II, III, I
    C. III, I, II   D. III, II, I

25. The temperature of the returning condensate in a low-pressure steam heating system is   25.____
195° F.
This temperature indicates that

    A. some radiator traps are defective
    B. some boiler tubes are leaking
    C. the boiler water level is too low
    D. there is a high vacuum in the return line

26. An over-the-fire draft gauge in a natural draft furnace is USUALLY read in   26.____

    A. feet per minute   B. pounds per square inch
    C. inches of mercury   D. inches of water

27. The Air Pollution Code states that no person shall cause or permit the emission of an air   27.____
contaminant of a density which appears as dark or darker than number _____ on the
standard smoke chart.

    A. one   B. two   C. three   D. four

28. The equipment which is used to provide tempered fresh air to certain areas of a school building is a(n)　　28.____

    A.　exhaust fan   B.　window fan
    C.　fixed louvre   D.　heating stack

29. When a glass globe is put back over a newly replaced lightbulb in a ceiling light fixture, the holding screws on the globe should be tightened, then loosened, one half turn. This is done MAINLY to prevent　　29.____

    A.　fires caused by electrical short circuits
    B.　cracking of the globe due to heat expansion
    C.　falling of the globe from the light fixture
    D.　building up of harmful gases inside the globe

30. Standard 120 volt type fuses are GENERALLY rated in　　30.____

    A.　farads   B.　ohms   C.　watts   D.　amperes

31. A cleaner informs you that his electric vacuum cleaner is not working even though he tried the off-on switch several times and checked to see that the plug was still in the wall outlet.
Of the following, the FIRST course of action you should take in this situation is to　　31.____

    A.　determine if the circuit breaker has tripped out
    B.　take apart the vacuum cleaner
    C.　replace the electric cord on the vacuum cleaner
    D.　replace the electrical outlet

32. The one of the following that is the MOST practical method for a school custodian to use in making a temporary repair in a straight portion of a water pipe which has a small leak is to　　32.____

    A.　attach a clamped patch over the leak
    B.　weld or braze the pipe, depending on the material
    C.　drill and tap the pipe, then insert a plug
    D.　fill the hole with an epoxy sealer

33. The PRIMARY function of the packing which is generally found in the stuffing box of a centrifugal pump is to　　33.____

    A.　compensate for misalignment of the pump shaft
    B.　prevent leakage of the fluid
    C.　control the discharge rate of the pump
    D.　provide support for the pump shaft

34. Of the following, the MOST important reason for replacing a worn washer in a dripping faucet as soon as possible is to prevent　　34.____

    A.　overflow of the sink trap
    B.　the mixture of hot and cold water in the sink
    C.　damage to the faucet parts that can be the result of overtightening the stem
    D.　air from entering the supply line

35. In carpentry work, the MOST commonly used hand saw is the _____ saw.   35.____

    A. hack   B. rip   C. buck   D. cross-cut

36. The device which USUALLY keeps a doorknob from rotating on the spindle is a   36.____

    A. cotter pin   B. tapered key
    C. set screw   D. stop screw

37. The following tasks are frequently done when an office is cleaned: 37.____
        I.   The floor is vacuumed
        II. The ashtrays and wastebaskets are emptied
        III. The desks and furniture are dusted
    The order in which these tasks should GENERALLY be done is

    A. I, II, III   B. II, III, I
    C. III, II, I   D. I, III, II

38. When wax is applied to a floor by the use of a twine mop with a handle, the wax should   38.____
    be _____ with the mop.

    A. applied in thin coats
    B. applied in heavy coats
    C. poured on the floor, then spread
    D. dripped on the floor, then spread

39. The BEST way to clean dust from an acoustical type ceiling is with a   39.____

    A. strong soap solution   B. wet sponge
    C. vacuum cleaner   D. stream of water

40. Of the following, the MOST important reason why a wet mop should NOT be wrung out   40.____
    by hand is that

    A. the strings of the mop will be damaged by hand-wringing
    B. sharp objects picked up by the mop may injure the hands
    C. the mop cannot be made dry enough by hand-wringing
    D. fine dirt will become embedded in the strings of the mop

KEY (CORRECT ANSWERS)

1.	A	11.	B	21.	B	31.	A
2.	C	12.	C	22.	C	32.	A
3.	B	13.	B	23.	A	33.	B
4.	A	14.	A	24.	B	34.	C
5.	B	15.	D	25.	A	35.	D
6.	B	16.	B	26.	D	36.	C
7.	D	17.	C	27.	D	37.	B
8.	A	18.	A	28.	B	38.	A
9.	D	19.	C	29.	B	39.	C
10.	A	20.	B	30.	D	40.	B

TEST 2

DIRECTIONS: Each question or incomplete statement is followed by several suggested answers or completions. Select the one that BEST answers the question or completes the statement. *PRINT THE LETTER OF THE CORRECT ANSWER IN THE SPACE AT THE RIGHT.*

1. When a painted wall is washed by hand, the wall should be washed from the _____ with a _____ sponge.   1._____

    A. top down; soaking wet
    B. bottom up; soaking wet
    C. top down; damp
    D. bottom up; damp

2. When a painted wall is brushed with a clean lambswool duster, the duster should be drawn _____ with _____ pressure.   2._____

    A. downward; light
    B. upward; light
    C. downward; firm
    D. upward; firm

3. The one of the following terms which BEST describes the size of a floor brush is   3._____

    A. 72 cubic inch
    B. 32 ounce
    C. 24 inch
    D. 10 square foot

4. When a slate blackboard is washed by hand, it is BEST to use   4._____

    A. a mild soap solution and allow the blackboard to air dry
    B. warm water and allow the blackboard to air dry
    C. a mild soap solution and sponge the blackboard dry
    D. warm water and sponge the blackboard dry

5. The MAIN reason why the handle of a reversible floor brush should be shifted from one side of the brush block to the opposite side is to   5._____

    A. change the angle at which the brush sweeps the floor
    B. give equal wear to both sides of the brush
    C. permit the brush to sweep hard-to-reach areas
    D. make it easier to sweep backward

6. When a long corridor is swept with a floor brush, it is good practice to   6._____

    A. push the brush with moderately long strokes and flick it after each stroke
    B. press on the brush and push it the whole length of the corridor in one sweep
    C. pull the brush inward with short brisk strokes
    D. sweep across rather than down the length of the corridor

7. Of the following office cleaning jobs performed during the year, the one which should be done MOST frequently is   7._____

    A. cleaning the fluorescent lights
    B. dusting the Venetian blinds
    C. cleaning the bookcase glass
    D. carpet-sweeping the rug

8. The BEST polishing agent to use on wood furniture is   8.____

    A. pumice   B. paste wax
    C. water emulsion wax   D. neatfoot's oil

9. Lemon oil polish is used BEST to polish   9.____

    A. exterior bronze   B. marble walls
    C. lacquered metal floors   D. leather seats

10. Cleaning with trisodium phosphate will MOST likely damage   10.____

    A. toilet bowls   B. drain pipes
    C. polished marble floors   D. rubber tile floors

11. Of the following cleaning agents, the one which should NOT be used is   11.____

    A. caustic lye   B. detergent
    C. scouring powder   D. ammonia

12. The one of the following cleaners which GENERALLY contains an abrasive is   12.____

    A. caustic lye   B. trisodium phosphate
    C. scouring powder   D. ammonia

13. The instructions on a box of cleaning powder say, *Mix one pound of cleaning powder in four gallons of water.* According to these instructions, how many ounces of cleaning powder should be mixed in one gallon of water?   13.____

    A. 4   B. 8   C. 12   D. 16

14. In accordance with recommended practice, a dust mop, when not used, should be stored   14.____

    A. hanging, handle end down
    B. hanging, handle end up
    C. standing on the floor, handle end down
    D. standing on the floor, handle end up

15. The two types of floors found in public buildings are classified as *hard* and *soft* floors. An example of a hard floor is one made of   15.____

    A. linoleum   B. cork
    C. ceramic tile   D. asphalt tile

16. The BEST way for a custodian to determine whether a cleaner is doing his work well is by   16.____

    A. observing the cleaner at work for several hours
    B. asking the cleaner questions about the work
    C. asking other cleaners to rate his work
    D. inspecting the cleanliness of the spaces assigned to the cleaner

17. A chemical frequently used to melt ice on outdoor pavements is   17.____

    A. ammonia   B. soda
    C. carbon tetrachloride   D. calcium chloride

18. A herbicide is a chemical PRIMARILY used as a(n)

    A. disinfectant   B. fertilizer
    C. insect killer   D. weed killer

18.____

19. Established plants that continue to blossom year after year without reseeding are GEN-ERALLY known as

    A. annuals   B. parasites
    C. perennials   D. symbiotics

19.____

20. A ferrous sulfate solution is sometimes used to treat shrubs or trees that have a deficiency of

    A. boron   B. copper   C. iron   D. zinc

20.____

21. A tree is described as deciduous.
This means PRIMARILY that it

    A. bears nuts instead of fruit
    B. has been pruned recently
    C. usually grows in swampy ground
    D. loses its leaves in fall

21.____

22. If you are told that a container holds a 20-7-7 fertilizer, it is MOST likely that twenty percent of this fertilizer is

    A. nitrogen   B. oxygen
    C. phosphoric acid   D. potash

22.____

23. When the national flag is in such a worn condition that it is no longer a fitting emblem for display, it should be disposed of by

    A. bagging inconspicuously with other disposables
    B. burning in an inconspicuous place
    C. laundering and then using it for cleaning purposes
    D. storing for future use as a painter's dropcloth

23.____

24. The landscape drawings for a school indicate the planting of *Acer platanoides* at a certain location on the grounds. Acer platanoides is a type of

    A. privet hedge   B. rose bush
    C. maple tree   D. tulip bed

24.____

25. Improper use of a carbon dioxide type portable fire extinguisher may cause injury to the operator because

    A. handling the nozzle during discharge can cause frostbite to the skin
    B. carbon dioxide is highly poisonous if breathed into the lungs
    C. use of carbon dioxide on ah oil fire can cause a chemical explosion
    D. of the extremely high pressures inside the extinguisher

25.____

26. When using a portable single ladder with ten rungs, the GREATEST number of rungs that a cleaner should climb up is

    A. 7   B. 8   C. 9   D. 10

26.____

27. Of the following types of portable fire extinguishers, the one which should be used to control a fire in or around live electrical equipment is the _____ type.   27._____

    A. foam   B. soda acid
    C. carbon dioxide   D. gas cartridge water

28. The MOST frequent cause of accidental injuries to workers on the job is   28._____

    A. unsafe working practices of employees
    B. poor design of buildings and working areas
    C. lack of warning signs in hazardous working areas
    D. lack of adequate safety guards on equipment and machinery

29. Of the following, the MOST important purpose of preparing an accident report on an injury to a cleaner is to help   29._____

    A. collect statistics on different types of accidents
    B. calm the feelings of the injured cleaner
    C. prevent similar accidents in the future
    D. prove that the cleaner was at fault

30. A cleaner is attempting to lift a heavy drum of liquid cleaner from the floor to a shelf at waist height. He will MOST likely avoid personal injury in lifting the drum if he   30._____

    A. keeps his back as straight as possible and lifts the weight
    B. arches his back and lifts the weight primarily with his back muscles
    C. keeps his back as straight as possible and lifts the weight primarily with his leg muscles
    D. arches his back and lifts the weight primarily with his leg muscles

31. Of the following, the BEST first aid treatment for a cleaner who has burned his hand with dry caustic lye crystals is to   31._____

    A. wash his hand with large quantities of warm water
    B. brush his hand lightly with a soft, clean brush and wrap it in a clean rag
    C. place his hand in a mild solution of ammonia and cool water
    D. wash his hand with large quantities of cold water

32. The purpose of the third prong in a three-prong electric plug used on a 120-volt electric vacuum cleaner is to prevent   32._____

    A. serious overheating of the vacuum cleaner
    B. electric shock to the operator of the vacuum cleaner
    C. generation of dangerous microwaves by the vacuum cleaner
    D. sparking in the electric outlet caused by a loose electrical wire

33. Of the following, the LEAST effective method for a school custodian to use to reduce window glass breakage in his school is to   33._____

    A. keep the area near the school free of sticks and stones
    B. consult with parents and civic organizations and request their assistance in reducing breakage

C. request that neighbors living near the school report afterhours incidents to the police department
D. develop a reputation as a *tough guy* with the students so that they will be afraid to break windows in the school

34. The one of the following procedures that a school custodian should use when a telephone caller makes a threat to place a bomb in the school is to

    A. hang up on the caller
    B. keep the caller talking as long as possible and make notes on what he says
    C. tell the caller he has the wrong number
    D. tell the caller his voice is being recorded and the call is being traced to its source

34.___

35. A school custodian is responsible for enforcing certain safety regulations in the school. The MOST important reason for enforcing safety regulations is because

    A. every accident can be prevented
    B. compliance with safety regulations will make all other safety efforts unnecessary
    C. safety regulations are the law and law enforcement is an end in itself
    D. safety regulations are based on reason and experience with the best methods of accident prevention

35.___

36. The safety belts that are worn by cleaners when washing outside windows should be inspected

    A. before each use   B. weekly
    C. monthly   D. semi-annually

36.___

37. The one of the following actions that a school custodian should take to help reduce burglary losses in the school is to

    A. leave all the lights on in the school overnight
    B. see that interior and exterior doors are securely locked
    C. set booby traps that will severely injure anyone breaking in
    D. set up an apartment in the school basement and stay at the school every night

37.___

38. The one of the following types of locks that is used on emergency exit doors is a _____ bolt.

    A. panic   B. dead   C. cinch   D. toggle

38.___

39. A telephone caller tells a school custodian that a bomb has been placed in the building and immediately hangs up the phone.
The FIRST thing the school custodian should do, in the absence of the principal, is to

    A. call the fire department
    B. call the police department
    C. let his subordinate handle it
    D. ignore the call, since most threats are hoaxes

39.___

40. If an employee's bi-weekly salary is $1200.00 and 6.7% is withheld for taxes, the amount to be withheld for this purpose is MOST NEARLY

    A. $62.00   B. $66.00   C. $82.00   D. $74.00

40.___

KEY (CORRECT ANSWERS).

1.	D	11.	A	21.	D	31.	D
2.	A	12.	C	22.	A	32.	B
3.	C	13.	A	23.	B	33.	D
4.	B	14.	B	24.	C	34.	B
5.	B	15.	C	25.	A	35.	D
6.	A	16.	D	26.	B	36.	A
7.	D	17.	D	27.	C	37.	B
8.	B	18.	D	28.	A	38.	A
9.	A	19.	C	29.	C	39.	B
10.	C	20.	C	30.	C	40.	C

EXAMINATION SECTION
TEST 1

DIRECTIONS: Each question or incomplete statement is followed by several suggested answers or completions. Select the one that BEST answers the question or completes the statement. *PRINT THE LETTER OF THE CORRECT ANSWER IN THE SPACE AT THE RIGHT.*

1. Of the following, the BEST practice to follow in criticizing the work performance of a cleaner is to   1.____

    A. save up several criticisms and make them all at once
    B. soften your criticisms by being humorous
    C. have another cleaner, who has more seniority, give the criticism
    D. make sure that you explain to the cleaner the reasons for your criticisms

2. A group of students complains to you about the lack of cleanliness in the building. You realize that budget cutbacks have unavoidably led to shortages in manpower and equipment for the cleaning staff.
Of the following, the BEST way for you to answer these students is to   2.____

    A. tell them frankly that the cleanliness of the building is none of their business
    B. apologize for the condition of the building and promise that your men will work harder
    C. tell them to take their complaints to the administration and not to you
    D. explain the reason for the building's condition and what you are doing to improve it

3. Your supervisor has ordered you to announce to your cleaners a new cleaning rule with which you disagree. You should   3.____

    A. admit honestly to your cleaners that you disagree with the rule
    B. announce the rule to your cleaners without expressing your disagreement
    C. encourage your cleaners by telling them that you agree with the rule
    D. tell your supervisor that you refuse to announce any rule with which you disagree

4. The preparation of work schedules for custodial employees and the daily work routine of these employees is determined and regulated by the   4.____

    A. principal
    B. district supervisor of custodians
    C. chief of custodians
    D. school custodian

5. The records and reports of school plant operations are originated by the school custodian and forwarded on a monthly basis to the   5.____

    A. borough supervisor
    B. district superintendent
    C. director of plant operations
    D. chief of custodians

6. The operation, care, maintenance, and minor repair of a school building and grounds is   6.____
the duty and responsibility of the school custodian.
This responsibility

    A.   can be delegated to the custodial staff
    B.   is shared with the custodial staff
    C.   cannot be delegated and is the school custodian's only
    D.   is shared with the district supervisor

7. A cleaner does a very good job on the work assigned to him, but on several occasions   7.____
you find him lounging and reading a magazine in an isolated part of the building. The
BEST thing for you to do is

    A.   tell the man to increase the time it takes to do the job so as to reduce his lax time
    B.   give him a strong reprimand
    C.   check the log book or personnel records and confer with the staff and principal to
        see if there are any complaints against him
    D.   tell the man to report to you whenever he finishes the required work

8. If one of your employees approaches you with a suggestion on how to improve work pro-   8.____
cedures, you should

    A.   ignore it
    B.   listen to the suggestion and take appropriate action
    C.   refer the employee to the principal
    D.   tell the employee to tell the union

9. When instructing a new employee, you should include all of the following EXCEPT   9.____

    A.   the shortcomings, failures, and attitudes of fellow workers
    B.   unusual situations and hazardous conditions of work assignments
    C.   the normal hours of employment and special situations which require overtime
    D.   the rules, regulations, customs, and policies of the assignment

10. You are newly assigned to a building in which the custodial staff has been working effec-   10.____
tively for many years. In order to obtain the respect of the staff, you should

    A.   immediately make major significant changes in procedures to establish your
        authority
    B.   immediately make minor changes to show that you have new ideas, plans, and
        organizational ability
    C.   criticize your predecessor to establish your identity, attitude, and authority
    D.   make no changes to work schedules or assignments until you are fully aware of
        the existing practices, schedules, and assignments

11. Suppose that a cleaner has been found to be quite negligent in his work and has been   11.____
warned repeatedly by you. If you find that your warnings have not changed the man's
attitude or work habits, the PROPER thing to do is to

    A.   discharge the employee
    B.   change his assignment in the school to a less desirable job
    C.   have a serious talk with the cleaner to find out why he does not do satisfactory
        work
    D.   give the cleaner a final warning

12. An after-school play center is in operation in your building. On a particular afternoon, the children in this activity are especially noisy and creating a disturbance.
The FIRST procedure to follow is to

12.____

    A. notify the day school principal of this situation
    B. notify the teacher in charge of this situation
    C. pay no attention to this situation and forget about it
    D. notify the police

13. A school custodian is required to submit several types of written reports to his supervisor on a monthly basis. After submitting his monthly reports, a custodian discovers he has made an error.
The CORRECT procedure for the school custodian to follow concerning this matter is to

13.____

    A. notify the supervisor and have the supervisor correct the error
    B. notify the supervisor and request the return of the report so that the custodian can correct the error
    C. take no action so that the error may be unnoticed
    D. take no action so that the supervisor may find the mistake

14. New cleaning materials are constantly appearing on the market.
It would be ADVISABLE for the custodian engineer to

14.____

    A. sample them to determine the cost factor
    B. trial test in an operation
    C. check materials for product safety
    D. all of the above

15. All vacuum tubes in oil burner programmers, smoke detection devices, and other electronic controls should be changed

15.____

    A. as needed   B. monthly
    C. yearly   D. every 3 years

16. In the event of flame failure, what occurs FIRST?

16.____

    A. Magnetic oil valve closes.
    B. Metering valve reduces oil flow.
    C. Magnetic gas valve closes.
    D. Primary air supply is closed.

17. A burner mounted vaporstat is a control used in conjunction with proving

17.____

    A. ignition   B. proper oil temperature
    C. flame failure   D. primary air

18. Secondary air dampers on a boiler with a rotary cup oil burner are installed PRIMARILY to

18.____

    A. measure the flow of air into the furnace
    B. furnish air for atomization
    C. furnish air for combustion
    D. regulate boiler steam pressure

19. In a fully automatic oil burning plant, ignition of fuel oil in the firebox is accomplished by   19.____

    A. spark ignition
    B. hand torch
    C. kerosene rags
    D. spark ignition which ignites a gas pilot

20. The purpose of recirculating fuel oil is PRIMARILY to   20.____

    A. bring it up to the proper temperature
    B. heat oil in storage tanks
    C. force out air
    D. bring oil up to burner

21. The atomization of the oil in a rotary cup oil burner is PRIMARILY due to   21.____

    A. oil pressure
    B. rotary cup *only*
    C. secondary air
    D. rotary cup and primary air

22. A rotary cup oil burner is started and stopped by means of the   22.____

    A. magnetic oil valve   B. modutrol motor
    C. pressuretrol   D. vaporstat

23. The fuel oil suction strainer outside the oil storage tanks should be cleaned when   23.____

    A. burner flame fluctuates
    B. steam pressure drops
    C. flame failure occurs
    D. a differential in vacuum reading across strainer occurs

24. The LOWEST temperature at which oil gives off sufficient vapors to explode momentarily, when flame is applied, is known as _____ point.   24.____

    A. flash   B. fire
    C. pour   D. atomization

25. Air/oil ratio in a rotary cup burner is correctly arrived at with the proper setting of the following: 25.____

    A. Aquastat, vaporstat, pressurestat
    B. Metering valve, primary air, pressurestat
    C. Metering valve, primary air, secondary air
    D. Aquastat, primary air, secondary air

KEY (CORRECT ANSWERS)

1. D	11. A
2. D	12. B
3. B	13. B
4. D	14. D
5. A	15. C
6. C	16. A
7. D	17. D
8. B	18. C
9. A	19. D
10. D	20. A

21. D
22. C
23. D
24. A
25. C

———

TEST 2

DIRECTIONS: Each question or incomplete statement is followed by several suggested answers or completions. Select the one that BEST answers the question or completes the statement. *PRINT THE LETTER OF THE CORRECT ANSWER IN THE SPACE AT THE RIGHT.*

1. The school custodian can help create goodwill and cooperation by the students, faculty, parents, visitors, and the general public through

   A. minding his own business
   B. carrying out his duties diligently
   C. reporting all infractions to the principal
   D. letting his supervisor worry about building operations

1.____

2. The school custodian has as his responsibility all of the following equipment EXCEPT

   A. that used for educational and/or culinary purposes
   B. electrical
   C. swimming pool machinery
   D. elevator and sidewalk hoist equipment

2.____

3. Upon hiring, custodial employees are required to be

   A. x-rayed or tine tested
   B. fingerprinted and police checked
   C. issued ID cards by personnel security
   D. all of the above

3.____

4. *Minor* repairs consist of

   A. mechanical adjustment and repacking
   B. clearing minor stoppages and limited glazing
   C. tightening and temporary repairs
   D. all of the above

4.____

5. Plant operation of the Board of Education is a bureau within the

   A. Division of School Buildings
   B. Office of Design and Construction
   C. Office of Business Affairs
   D. Bureau of Maintenance

5.____

6. Of the following ways of improving the success of a safety program, the one MOST likely to secure employee acceptance and interest is

   A. frequent inspection
   B. employee participation in the program
   C. posting attractive notices in work areas and employee quarters
   D. frequent meetings of employees at which safe methods are demonstrated

6.____

7. With regard to supplies, a good procedure is to utilize a daily inventory.   7.____
   The reason for this is that

   A. you are aware of what is on hand at all times
   B. you know if anyone is stealing
   C. it keeps you busy
   D. you can check and see if your employees are working

8. A school custodian notices a man in a corridor. This visitor identifies himself as a police   8.____
   officer and states he is observing a student in one of the classes.
   The school custodian should

   A. make no further inquiries
   B. ask if the police officer has checked with the school principal
   C. ask for details—the name of the student, reason for observations, etc.—so as to
      make a log book entry
   D. ask the officer to leave unless he has written permission from the principal

9. In filling out an accident report on an injured cleaner, the LEAST important item to   9.____
   include in the report is the

   A. equipment being used when the injury occurred
   B. attitude of the cleaner towards his job
   C. nature and extent of the injury
   D. work being done when the accident occurred

10. A dispute arises with a cleaner regarding his duties, where he claims the work assigned   10.____
    is *not his job*. After explaining his duties to him and showing him his work schedule, he
    still refuses to perform the disputed duties. To resolve this difficulty, you would

    A. fire him for insubordination
    B. notify the school principal
    C. call in the employees union delegate
    D. call in the district supervisor of custodians

11. A number of pupil injuries have occurred while they were traveling on school stairs. Your   11.____
    inspection shows no defects or inadequacy of lighting.
    The MOST desirable step to take to reduce the frequency of these accidents is to

    A. assign a cleaner to each stairway when being used
    B. put up signs warning children to be careful
    C. discuss the matter with the school principal
    D. install better stair lighting and make sure handrails are in perfect order

12. The *fuel and utility* report is a record of fuel and electricity used in a school building.   12.____
    This report should be sent to the administrative supervisor

    A. daily   B. weekly   C. monthly   D. yearly

13. One of your employees is constantly dissatisfied and is always complaining.   13.___
    The BEST procedure to follow regarding this man is to

    A. reprimand him and warn him that his conduct is affecting the other employees and
       that unless he changes his attitude he will be dismissed
    B. reassign him to a job where he will be more closely supervised
    C. discuss in detail his dissatisfaction and determine the cause
    D. supervise him less closely

14. Custodial payroll reports are submitted   14.___

    A. every two weeks   B. every four weeks
    C. monthly   D. quarterly

15. An inventory of capital equipment must be filled out   15.___

    A. monthly
    B. upon change of custodians
    C. semi-annually
    D. yearly

16. School custodians are required to inspect their buildings for fire prevention and fire   16.___
    safety

    A. daily   B. weekly   C. monthly   D. quarterly

17. A contractor working in your building is doing unsatisfactory repair work.   17.___
    You would notify, in writing, the

    A. borough or administrative supervisor
    B. district superintendent
    C. contract compliance division
    D. director of plant operations

18. If one of your employees frequently misplaces cleaning equipment, you would   18.___

    A. notify the borough supervisor
    B. handle the problem yourself
    C. call in the chief of custodians to speak to the employee
    D. tell the principal of the school and ask for action against the employee

19. Safety education of custodial employees is the direct responsibility of the   19.___

    A. school custodian
    B. principal
    C. borough supervisor
    D. director of plant operations

20. Worker's compensation insurance coverage for custodial employees is provided by all   20.___
    of the following EXCEPT the

    A. board of education   B. union
    C. school custodian   D. school

21. Request for plumbing repairs which cannot be performed by the custodial staff are for-   21.____
   warded to the

   A. chief of custodians
   B. director of plant operations
   C. borough supervisor
   D. plumbing shops

22. The cleaning of electrical distribution panel boxes and switchboards is the responsibility   22.____
   of the

   A. principal   B. school custodian
   C. district supervisor   D. cleaner

23. A parent complains that one of your cleaners used abusive language to him.   23.____
   As the school custodian, you should

   A. reprimand the cleaner
   B. fire the cleaner
   C. investigate the complaint to find out if there is any basis to the allegation
   D. ignore the complaint

24. Of the following, the LARGEST individual item of custodial expense in operating a school   24.____
   building is generally the cost of

   A. labor   B. fuel
   C. electricity   D. elevator services

25. A telephone caller tells a school custodian that a bomb has been placed in the building   25.____
   and immediately hangs up the phone.
   The FIRST thing the school custodian should do, in the absence of the principal, is to

   A. call the fire department
   B. call the police department
   C. let the principal's subordinate handle it
   D. ignore the call since most threats are hoaxes

————————

KEY (CORRECT ANSWERS)

1.	B		11.	C
2.	A		12.	C
3.	D		13.	C
4.	D		14.	B
5.	A		15.	D
6.	B		16.	A
7.	A		17.	A
8.	B		18.	B
9.	B		19.	A
10.	A		20.	B

21.	C
22.	B
23.	C
24.	A
25.	B

———

BASIC FUNDAMENTALS OF BOILERS
CONTENTS

BASIC FUNDAMENTALS OF BOILERS

I. NATURE

The boiler is the source or high-temperature region of the thermo-dynamic cycle. The steam that is generated in the boiler is led to the turbines, where its thermal energy is converted into mechanical energy (work) which drives the unit and provides power for vital services.

In essence, a boiler is merely a container in which water can be boiled and steam generated. A tea kettle on a stove is basically a boiler, although a rather inefficient one. Note that the steam is generated in one vessel and superheated in another, since it is impossible to raise the temperature of the steam above the temperature of the boiling water as long as the two are in contact with each other.

In designing a boiler which must produce a large amount of steam, it is obviously necessary to find some means of providing a larger amount of heat-transfer surface than could be provided by a vessel shaped like a tea kettle. In most modern boilers, the steam generating surface consists of hundreds and hundreds of tubes, which provide a maximum amount of heat-transfer surface in a relatively small space. As a rule, the tubes communicate with a steam drum at the top of a boiler and with water drums and headers at the bottom of the boiler. The tubes and part of the drums are enclosed in an insulated casing which has space inside it for the furnace. A boiler appears to be a fairly complicated piece of equipment when it is considered with all its fittings, piping, and accessories; it may be helpful, therefore, to remember that the basic components of a saturated-steam boiler are merely the tubes, the drums, and headers, and the furnace.

Practically all boilers used in propulsion are designed to produce both saturated steam and superheated steam. To our basic boiler, therefore, we must now add another component: the superheater. The superheater on most boilers consists of headers, usually located at the back of the boiler, and a number of superheater tubes which communicate with the headers. Saturated steam from the steam drum is led through the superheater; since the steam is now no longer in contact with the water from which it was generated, the steam becomes superheated as additional heat is supplied. In some boilers there is a separate superheater furnace; in others, the superheater tubes project into the same furnace that is used for the generation of saturated steam.

Some question may arise concerning the need for both saturated steam and superheated steam. Saturated steam is used for operating most steamdriven auxiliary machinery; reciprocating machinery, in particular, requires saturated steam for the lubrication of the moving parts of the steam end. Superheated steam is used almost exclusively for the propulsion turbines. There is more available energy in superheated steam than in saturated steam at the same pressure; and the use of higher temperatures vastly increases the efficiency of the propulsion cycle since, as we have seen, the efficiency of a heat engine is dependent upon the absolute temperature at the source (boiler) and the absolute temperature at the receiver (condenser). In some instances, the gain in efficiency resulting from the use of superheated steam may be as much as 15 percent for 200 degrees of superheat. This increase in efficiency is particularly important because it allows substantial savings in fuel consumption and in space and weight requirements. A further advantage in using superheated steam for propulsion machinery is that it causes relatively little erosion or corrosion since it is free of moisture.

II. CLASSIFICATION

Boilers may be classified in a number of different ways, according to various design features. Most commonly, they are classified and described in terms of (1) the relative location of the fire and water spaces, (2) the size of the tubes, (3) the type of circulation, and (4) the type of superheat. Some knowledge of these methods of classification will be useful in understanding the design and construction of modern boilers.

A. Location of Fire and Water Spaces

First of all, boilers are classified according to the relative location of their fire and water spaces. By this classification, all, boilers may be divided into two groups: *fire-tube boilers* and *water-tube boilers*. In *fire-tube boilers,* the gases of combustion flow through the tubes and thereby heat the surrounding water. In *water-tube boilers,* the water flows through the tubes and is heated by the gases of combustion that fill the furnace.

B. Size of Tubes

Water-tube boilers are further classified according to the size of the tubes. Boilers having tubes 2 inches or more in diameter are called *large-tube boilers*. Boilers having tubes less than 2 inches in diameter are called *small-tube* or *express-type boilers*.

C. Type of Circulation

Water-tube boilers are also classified as *natural circulation boilers* or as *forced circulation boilers,* depending upon the way in which the water circulates within the boiler.

Natural circulation boilers are those in which the circulation of water depends upon the difference in density between an ascending mixture of hot water and steam and a descending body of relatively cool and steam-free water. Natural circulation may be of two types, free or accelerated.

In this type of boiler, the generating tubes are installed at a slight angle of inclination which allows the lighter hot water and steam to rise while the cooler (and heavier) water descends.

Installing the generating tubes at a greater angle of inclination increases the rate of water circulation. Hence, boilers in which the tubes slope more steeply are said to have accelerated natural circulation.

Most modern boilers are designed for accelerated natural circulation. In such boilers, large tubes (3 or more inches in diameter) are installed between the steam drum and the water drums. These tubes, called *downcomers,* are located outside the furnace and away from the heat of combustion, thereby serving as pathways for the downward flow of relatively cool water. When a sufficient number of downcomers are installed, all small tubes can be generating tubes, carrying steam and water upward; and all downward flow can be carried by the downcomers. The size and number of downcomers installed varies from one type of boiler to another.

Forced circulation boilers are, as their name implies, quite different in design from the boilers that utilize natural circulation. Instead of depending upon differences in density between the hotter and the cooler water, forced circulation boilers use pumps to force the water through the various boiler circuits. Forced circulation boilers are relatively new, but they have some very definite advantages which will probably lead to their increased use in the future.

D. Type of Superheat

Practically all boilers are equipped with superheaters. With respect to the superheater installation, boilers are classified as having either controlled superheat or uncontrolled superheat. In a boiler with *controlled superheat,* the degree of superheat can be changed by regulating the amount of heat supplied to the superheater tube bank, without substantially changing the amount of heat supplied to the generating tubes. This control of superheat is possible because the boiler has two furnaces, one for the saturated side and one for the superheat side. A boiler with *uncontrolled superheat,* on the other hand, has only one furnace; and since the same furnace must be used for heating both the generating tubes and the superheater tubes, the degree of superheat cannot be controlled but varies within a small range as a function of design and firing rate.

Various terms are used to describe these two basic types of superheaters. Where the superheat is controlled, the superheater is often referred to as an *integral, separately fired superheat,* and the boiler as a whole is called a *superheat control boiler.* Where the superheat is not controlled, the superheater may be called an *integral, not separately fired superheater,* or it may be referred to as a *no control, or uncontrolled superheater;* and the boiler as a whole is called a *no control* or *uncontrolled superheat boiler.* The term *integral* is used to indicate that the superheater is installed as a part of the boiler unit. Practically all superheaters on modern boilers are integral with the boilers.

On both controlled and uncontrolled superheat boilers, the superheater tubes are protected from radiant heat by generating tubes that are called *water screen tubes .* The water screen tubes absorb the intense radiant heat of the furnace, and the superheater tubes are heated by convection currents rather than by direct radiation. Hence, the superheaters are sometimes called *convection-type superheaters.*

Some older types of superheat control boilers had *radiant-type superheaters* - that is, the superheater tubes were not screened by water tubes but were exposed directly to the radiant heat of the furnace. However, this type of superheater is relatively uncommon at the present time and will, therefore, not be further discussed.

III. TERMINOLOGY

In order to ensure uniform use of terms, there has been established a number of standard terms and definitions pertaining to boilers. Some of the more important of these definitions are given below.

A. Fire Room and Boiler Room - A compartment which contains boilers and the station for operating them is called a *fire room*. A compartment which contains boilers which does not contain the station for operating them is called a *boiler room.*

B. Boiler Emergency Station - This term is used to designate a station which is so located that, in the event of trouble, one may proceed with minimum delay to any fire room, boiler operating station, or boiler room.

C. Boiler Full-Power Capacity - The total quantity of steam required to develop contract shaft horsepower of the vessel, divided by the number of boilers installed, gives boiler full-power capacity. The quantity of steam is given in pounds of water evaporated per hour. Full-power capacity is indicated in the manufacturer's technical manual for each boiler.

D. Boiler Overload Capacity - Boiler overload capacity is specified in the design of the boiler. It is given in terms of steaming rate or firing rate, depending upon the individual installation. Boiler overload capacity is usually 120 percent of boiler full-power capacity.

E. Superheater Outlet Pressure - This is the actual steam pressure at the superheater outlet.

F. Steam Drum Pressure - This is the pressure in the steam drum. Steam drum pressure is specified in the design of a boiler and is given in the manufacturer's technical manual for each boiler. Steam drum pressure is the pressure which must be carried in the boiler steam drum in order to obtain the required pressure at the turbine throttles, when steaming at full-power capacity. Ordinarily, the designed steam drum pressure is carried for all steaming conditions.

G. Design Pressure - Design pressure is the pressure specified by the boiler manufacturer as a criterion for boiler design. It is usually 103 percent of steam drum pressure.

H. Operating Pressure - Operating pressure is the pressure at the final outlet from a boiler, after steam has passed through all baffles, the dry pipe, the superheater, etc., when the boiler is steaming at full-power capacity. Operating pressure is specified in the design of a boiler and is given in the manufacturer's technical manual. Operating pressure is the same as superheater outlet pressure when the boiler is steaming at full-power capacity; when the boiler is steaming at less than full-power capacity, however, the actual pressure at the superheater outlet will vary from the specified operating pressure provided a constant drum pressure is maintained.

I. Boiler Efficiency - The efficiency of a boiler is the British thermal units per pound of fuel absorbed by the water and steam divided by the British thermal units per pound of fuel fired. In other words, boiler efficiency is output divided by input, or Btu utilized divided by Btu available. Boiler efficiency is expressed as a percentage.

J. Fire Room Efficiency - The boiler efficiency corrected for blower and pump steam consumption is known as fire room efficiency. (This is not the same as boiler plant efficiency or propulsion plant efficiency.)

K. Total Heating Surface - The total heating surface of any steam generating unit consists of that portion of the heat transfer apparatus which is exposed on one side to the gases of combustion and on the other side to the water or steam being heated. Thus, the total heating surface equals the sum of the generating surface, the superheater surface, and the economizer surface. All heating surfaces are measured on the combustion-gas side.

L. Generating Surface - The generating surface is that portion of the total heating surface in which the fluid being heated forms part of the circulating system. The generating surface includes the boiler tube banks, water walls, water screens, and water floors (where installed and not covered by refractory material.)

M. Superheater Surface - The superheater surface is that portion of the total heating surface where the steam is heated after leaving the boiler steam drum.

N. Economizer Surface - The economizer surface is that portion of the total heating surface where the feed water is heated before entering the generating system.

O. Steaming Hours - The term steaming hours includes the time during which the boiler has fires lighted for raising steam and the time during which it is generating steam. Time during which fires are not lighted is not included in steaming hours.

GLOSSARY OF PLUMBING TERMS

TABLE OF CONTENTS

GLOSSARY OF PLUMBING TERMS

A

ACCEPTED STANDARDS

Accepted standards are the standards cited in the manual, or other standards approved by the authority having jurisdiction over plumbing.

AIR GAP

The air gap in a water-supply system for plumbing fixtures is the vertical distance between the supply-fitting outlet (spout) and the highest possible water level in the receptor when flooded.

If the plane at the end of the spout is at an angle to the surface of the water, the mean gap is the basis for measurement.

APPROVED

Approved means accepted as satisfactory to the authority having jurisdiction over plumbing.

AREA DRAIN

An area drain is a drain installed to collect surface or rain water from an open area.

B

BACKFLOW

Backflow means the flow of water into a water-supply system from any source except its regular one. Back siphonage is one type of backflow.

BACKFLOW CONNECTION

A backflow connection is any arrangement whereby backflow can occur.

BACK VENT

A back vent is a branch vent installed primarily for the purpose of protecting fixture traps from self-siphonage.

BRANCH

A branch is any part of a piping system other than a main. (See Main.)

BRANCH INTERVAL

A branch interval is a length of soil or waste stack corresponding in general to a story height, but in no case less than 8 feet, within which the horizontal branches from one floor or story of the building are connected to the stack.

BRANCH VENT

A branch vent is any vent pipe connecting from a branch of the drainage system to the vent stack.

BUILDING DRAIN

The building (house) drain is that part of the lowest horizontal piping of a building-drainage system which receives the discharge from soil, waste, and other drainage pipes inside the walls of the building and conveys it to the building (house) sewer beginning 5 feet outside the inner face of the building wall.

BUILDING-DRAINAGE SYSTEM

The building-drainage system consists of all piping provided for carrying waste water, sewage, or other drainage from the building to the street sewer or place of disposal.

BUILDING MAIN

The building main is the water-supply pipe including fittings and accessories, from the water (street) main or other source of supply to the first branch of the water-distributing system.

BUILDING SEWER

The building (house) sewer is that part of the horizontal piping of a building-drainage system extending from the building drain 5 feet outside of the inner face of the building wall to the street sewer or other place of disposal (a cesspool, septic tank, or other type of sewage-treatment device or devices) and conveying the drainage of but one building site.

BUILDING SUBDRAIN

A building (house) subdrain is that portion of a drainage system which cannot drain by gravity into the building sewer.

C

CIRCUIT VENT

A circuit vent is a group vent extending from in front of the last fixture connection of a horizontal branch to the vent stack.

COMBINATION FIXTURE

Combination fixture is a trade term designating an integral combination of one sink and one or two laundry trays in one fixture.

CONTINUOUS-WASTE-AND-VENT

A continuous-waste-and-vent is a vent that is a continuation of and in a straight line with the drain to which it connects. A continuous-waste-and-vent is further defined by the angle of the drain and vent at the point of connection make with the horizontal; for example, vertical continuous-waste-and-vent, 45 continuous-waste-and-vent, and flat (small angle) continuous-waste-and-vent.

CONTINUOUS WASTE

A waste from two or more fixtures connected to a single trap.

CROSS-CONNECTION

See: INTERCONNECTION

D

DEVELOPED LENGTH
The developed length of a pipe is its length along the center line of the pipe and fittings.

DIAMETER
Unless specifically stated, the term diameter means the nominal diameter as designated commercially.

DISTANCE
The distance or difference in elevation between two sloping pipes is the distance between the intersection of their center lines with the center line of the pipe to which both are connected.

DOUBLE OFFSET
A double offset is two offsets installed in succession or series in the same line.

DRAIN
A drain or drain pipe is any pipe which carries water or waterborne wastes in a building-drainage system.

DRAINAGE PIPING
Drainage piping is all or any part of the drain pipes of a plumbing system.

DRY VENT
A dry vent is any vent that does not carry water or water-borne wastes.

DUAL VENT
A dual vent (sometimes called a unit vent) is a group vent connecting at the junction of two fixture branches and serving as a back vent for both branches.

E

EFFECTIVE OPENING
The effective opening is the minimum cross-sectional area between the end of the supply-fitting outlet (spout) and the inlet to the controlling valve or faucet. The basis of measurement is the diameter of a circle of equal cross-sectional area.

If two or more lines supply one outlet, the effective opening is the sum of the effective openings of the individual lines or the area of the combined outlet, whichever is the smaller.

F

FIXTURE BRANCH
A fixture branch is the supply pipe between the fixture and the water-distributing pipe.

FIXTURE DRAIN
A fixture drain is the drain from the trap of a fixture to the junction of the drain with any other drain pipe.

FIXTURE UNIT
A fixture unit is a factor so chosen that the load-producing values of the different plumbing fixtures can be expressed approximately as multiples of that factor.

FLOOD LEVEL

Flood level in reference to a plumbing fixture is the level at which water begins to overflow the top or rim of the fixture.

G

GRADE

The grade of a line of pipe is its slope in reference to a horizontal plane. In plumbing it is usually expressed as the fall in inches per foot length of pipe.

GROUP VENT

A group vent is a branch vent that performs its functions for two or more traps.

H

HORIZONTAL BRANCH

A horizontal branch is a branch drain extending laterally from a soil or waste stack or building drain, with or without vertical sections or branches, which receives the discharge from one or more fixture drains and conducts it to the soil or waste stack or the building (house) drain.

I

INDIRECT WASTE PIPE

An indirect waste pipe is a waste pipe which does not connect directly with the building-drainage system, but discharges into it through a properly trapped fixture or receptacle.

INTERCONNECTION

An interconnection, as the term is used is any physical connection or arrangement of pipes between two otherwise separate building water-supply systems whereby water may flow from one system to the other, the direction of flow depending upon the pressure differential between the two systems.

Where such connection occurs between the sources of two such systems and the first branch from either, whether inside or outside the building, the term cross-connection (American Water Works terminology) applies and is generally used.

J

JUMPOVER

See: RETURN OFFSET.

L

LEADER

A leader or downspout is the water conductor from the roof to the storm drain or other means of disposal.

LOOP VENT

A loop vent is the same as a circuit vent except that it loops back and connects with a soil- or waste-stack vent instead of the vent stack.

M

MAIN

The main of any system of continuous piping is the principal artery of the system to which branches may be connected.

MAIN VENT

See: VENT STACK.

N

NONPRESSURE DRAINAGE

Nonpressure drainage refers to a condition in which a static pressure cannot be imposed safely on the building drain. This condition is sometimes referred to as gravity flow and implies that the sloping pipes are not completely filled.

O

OFFSET

An offset in a line of piping is a combination of elbows or bends which brings one section of the pipe out of line with but into a line parallel with another section.

P

PLUMBING

Plumbing is the work or business of installing in buildings the pipes, fixtures, and other apparatus for bringing in the water supply and removing liquid and water-borne wastes. The term is also used to denote the installed fixtures and piping of a building.

PLUMBING FIXTURES

Plumbing fixtures are receptacles which receive and discharge water, liquid, or water-borne wastes into a drainage system with which they are connected.

PLUMBING SYSTEM

The plumbing system of a building includes the water-supply distributing pipes; the fixtures and fixture traps; the soil, waste, and vent pipes; the building (house) drain and building (house) sewer; and the storm-drainage pipes; with their devices, appurtenances, and connections all within or adjacent to the building.

POOL

A pool is a water receptacle used for swimming or as a plunge or other bath, designed to accommodate more than one bather at a time.

PRESSURE DRAINAGE

Pressure drainage, as used in the manual, refers to a condition in which a static pressure may be imposed safely on the entrances of sloping building drains through soil and waste stacks connected thereto.

PRIMARY BRANCH

A primary branch of the building (house) drain is the single sloping drain from the base of a soil or waste stack to its junction with the main building drain or with another branch thereof.

R

RELIEF VENT

A relief vent is a branch from the vent stack, connected to a horizontal branch between the first fixture branch and the soil or waste stack, whose primary function is to provide for circulation of air between the vent stack and the solid or waste stack.

RETURN OFFSET

A return offset or jumpover is a double offset installed so as to return the pipe to its original line.

RISER

A riser is a water-supply pipe which extends vertically one full story or more to convey water to branches or fixtures.

S

SAND INTERCEPTOR (SAND TRAP)

A sand interceptor (sand trap) is a watertight receptacle designed and constructed to intercept and prevent the passage of sand or other solids into the drainage system to which it is directly or indirectly connected.

SANITARY SEWER

A sanitary sewer is a sewer designed or used only for conveying liquid or water-borne waste from plumbing fixtures.

SECONDARY BRANCH

A secondary branch of the building drain is any branch of the building drain other than a primary branch.

SEWAGE-TREATMENT PLANT

A sewage-treatment plant consists of structures and appurtenances which receive the discharge of a sanitary drainage system, designed to bring about a reduction in the organic and bacterial content of the waste so as to render it less offensive or dangerous, including septic tanks and cesspools.

SIDE VENT

A side vent is a vent connecting to the drain pipe through a 45° wye.

SIZE OF PIPE AND TUBING

The size of pipe or tubing, unless otherwise stated, is the nominal size by which the pipe or tubing is commercially designated. Actual dimensions of the different kinds of pipe and tubing are giver in the specifications applying.

SOIL PIPE

A soil pipe is any pipe which conveys the discharge of water closets or fixtures having similar functions, with or without the discharges from other fixtures.

STACK

Stack is a general term for the vertical main of a system of soil, waste, or vent piping.

STACK-VENT

A stack-vent is the extension of a soil or waste stack above the highest horizontal or fixture branch connected to the stack.

STORM DRAIN

A storm drain is a drain used for conveying rain water, subsurface water, condensate, cooling water, or other similar discharges.

STORM SEWER

A storm sewer is a sewer used for conveying rain water, subsurface water, condensate, cooling water, or other similar discharges.

SUBSOIL DRAIN

A subsoil drain is a drain installed for collecting subsurface or seepage water and conveying it to a place of disposal.

T

TRAP

A trap is a fitting or device so designed and constructed as to provide a liquid trap seal which will prevent the passage of air through it.

TRAP SEAL

The trap seal is the vertical distance between the crown weir and the dip of the trap.

V

VENT

A vent is a pipe installed to provide a flow of air to or from a drainage system or to provide a circulation of air within such system to protect trap seals from siphonage and back pressure.

VENT STACK

A vent stack, sometimes called a main vent, is a vertical vent pipe installed primarily for the purpose of providing circulation of air to or from any part of the building-drainage system.

W

WASTE PIPE

A waste pipe is a drain pipe which receives the discharge of any fixture other than water closets or other fixtures receiving human excreta.

WATER MAIN

The water (street) main is a water-supply pipe for public or community use.

WATER-SERVICE PIPE

The water-service pipe is that part of a building main installed by or under the jurisdiction of a water department or company.

WATER-SUPPLY SYSTEM

The water-supply system of a building consists of the water-service pipe, the water-distributing pipes, and the necessary connecting pipes, fittings, and control valves.

WET VENT

A wet vent is a soil or waste pipe that serves also as a vent.

Y

YOKE VENT

A yoke vent is a vertical or 45° relief vent of the continuous-waste-and-vent type formed by the extension of an upright wye-branch or 45° wye-branch inlet of the horizontal branch to the stack. It becomes a dual yoke vent when two horizontal branches are thus vented by the same relief vent.

ANSWER SHEET

TEST NO. _____ PART _____ TITLE OF POSITION _____

PLACE OF EXAMINATION _____ DATE___ _____

(CITY OR TOWN)　　　　　　　　　　　　　(STATE)

RATING

USE THE SPECIAL PENCIL.　MAKE GLOSSY BLACK MARKS.

1 2 3 4 5 6 7 8 9 10

26 27 28 29 30 31 32 33 34 35

51 52 53 54 55 56 57 58 59 60

76 77 78 79 80 81 82 83 84 85

101 102 103 104 105 106 107 108 109 110

Make only ONE mark for each answer.　Additional and stray marks may be counted as mistakes.　In making corrections, erase errors COMPLETELY.

11 12 13 14 15 16 17 18 19 20 21 22 23 24 25

36 37 38 39 40 41 42 43 44 45 46 47 48 49 50

61 62 63 64 65 66 67 68 69 70 71 72 73 74 75

86 87 88 89 90 91 92 93 94 95 96 97 98 99 100

111 112 113 114 115 116 117 118 119 120 121 122 123 124 125

ANSWER SHEET

TEST NO. _____ PART _____ TITLE OF POSITION _____
(AS GIVEN IN EXAMINATION ANNOUNCEMENT - INCLUDE OPTION, IF ANY)

PLACE OF EXAMINATION _____ DATE _____
(CITY OR TOWN)   (STATE)

RATING

USE THE SPECIAL PENCIL.   MAKE GLOSSY BLACK MARKS.

Make only ONE mark for each answer.   Additional and stray marks may be counted as mistakes.   In making corrections, erase errors COMPLETELY.